I0154166

Cyrus W. Hodgin

Outline of a Course of Study in United States History

With an introduction on the nature of the subject, the reasons for

teaching it, and the method of teaching it

Cyrus W. Hodgin

Outline of a Course of Study in United States History
With an introduction on the nature of the subject, the reasons for teaching it, and the method of teaching it

ISBN/EAN: 9783337381264

Printed in Europe, USA, Canada, Australia, Japan

Cover: Foto ©ninafisch / pixelio.de

More available books at **www.hansebooks.com**

OUTLINE

OF A

COURSE OF STUDY

IN

UNITED STATES HISTORY,

WITH AN INTRODUCTION ON THE NATURE OF THE SUBJECT, THE REASONS FOR TEACH-
ING IT, AND THE METHOD OF TEACHING IT; NOTES ON THE CIVILIZATION OF
THE ANCIENT MEXICANS AND PERUVIANS, AND ON THE PREPA-
RATION FOR THE DISCOVERY OF THE NEW WORLD.

By CYRUS W. HODGIN,

Teacher of History and Civil Government in the
State Normal School,

TERRE HAUTE, INDIANA,

"The roots of the present lie deep in the past, and nothing in
the past is dead to the man who would learn how the present comes
to be what it is."—*Stubbs*.

TERRE HAUTE, INDIANA:
PRINTED BY C. W. BROWN, AT THE GLOBE PRINTING OFFICE AND BINDERY.

1880.

PREFACE.

A few months ago the writer prepared and published for the use of his classes, a brief Outline of the work in United States History, as presented in the Normal School. The demand for it by those pupils who had gone out to teach, was so great, that the edition was soon exhausted. This revised edition has been prepared for the double purpose of supplying the classes in the Normal School, and of meeting the wants of those teachers who may find it useful to them in their schools.

The author desires to acknowledge his indebtedness to Ex-President, Wm. A. Jones, of the Normal School, for important hints and suggestions which, eight years ago, started him in the pleasant paths of historical investigation on a higher plane than he had before known.

He wishes also to express the pleasure he experiences as he recalls the patient industry and the quiet enthusiasm with which his many classes have worked with him in elaborating the matter of which this "Outline" has been the basis; and to them it is affectionately dedicated.

In the hope that it may stimulate to further research and to higher results, this edition is sent out to those for whom it is intended.   C. W. H.

Indiana State Normal School,
    Oct. 1, 1880.

INTRODUCTION.

The thoughtful and conscientious teacher, in beginning to give instruction in any subject, finds three questions presenting themselves to him and demanding clear and satisfactory answers:

1. *What* is it that I am to teach? What is the nature of the subject in itself considered? What are its limitations? How related to, and distinguished from, other kindred subjects?

2. *Why* am I to teach it? What are the uses to which it can be put by the learner? What is the end or purpose aimed at in giving instruction in it?

3. *How* am I to teach it? By what means and by what method can the end proposed be best secured?

The nature and relations of a subject determine the importance of knowing it; hence a comprehensive answer to the first question suggests an answer to the second.

The nature of a subject and the reasons for knowing it, largely determine the method of knowing it; hence the answers to the first and second questions, together with the nature of the mind, and the laws of its activity, furnish material for the answer to the third.

We shall briefly consider these questions as applied to History.

First, then, What is History?

The teacher should not be satisfied with a mere dictionary definition in answering this question for himself. While he must be able to give that in the best, clearest, and most comprehensive form, he must be able to do more. He must see the *subject itself* lying in his own mind with such clearness and distinctness, that he can present it to his classes in all its beauty, freshness, and living power.

Let the general idea of what History is, in its essential nature, be developed through the following propositions:

I. Every thing that was created was created for some end or purpose. Since an end or purpose is a thought, we must accept this proposition, or we deny the existence of intelligence.

II. The fulfilling of this end or purpose is the destiny of the created object. This is seen in material things; as, the mineral, the plant, the animal.

III. Man, as a spiritual being, is no exception to the law stated in proposition II.

IV. The final end or purpose of man is freedom; i.e., the realization of freedom is his destiny.

V. Man can achieve his destiny only through the organization of society. Man, isolated from organized society, lapses into barbarism. Said Aristotle, " Whoever lives voluntarily out of civil society must have a vicious disposition, or be an existence superior to man."

VI. The progress of mankind in the achievement of its destiny, is *History;* i.e., the history of the world is the development of the idea of freedom in the consciousness of mankind.

VII. In its broadest sense, History may be defined from two stand-points, one objective, the other subjective; and with reference to two classes of objects, natural and spiritual.

In the *objective* sense, History is the process of the development of nature and spirit.

In the *subjective* sense, it is the investigation and statement of the steps in the objective process.

NOTES.

Objective, as here used, means outer, external to the mind, which is the thinking subject. *Subjective*, inner, within the mind, brought under its activity or cognizance. The process of development, as of the acorn into an oak, may go on independently of the cognizance of any human mind; the process is objective, it is outer to the mind. When this process is brought under the cognizance of the mind; when it is investigated and stated, it then becomes subjective. This process as it lies within the mind is the subjective history of the oak.

A *process* is a moving or going forward, a method of proceeding.

A *Development* is the gradual unfolding of a plan or method through a series of progressive changes; through a succession of states or stages each of which is preparatory to the next. Or, it is the gradual realization, through a series of changes, of the *essence* of the *subject* of the development. The subject of the development in human history, is the human *spirit*, and the essence of spirit is freedom.

The *essence* of a thing is that property or quality of it upon which it depends for being what it is.

Spirit, the real man, as distinguished from his instrument, the body. Here the term is used rather in a general than in an individual sense, meaning the spirit of the race.

Investigation, literally the act of tracking or tracing.

A process of development necessarily implies change; change involves time, and implies the opposition of unequal forces. Not all change, however, implies development, and only those changes are of historical importance which promote the unfolding of the plan revealed in the process of development.

The realization on the part of spirit of its own essence comes through its own consciousness; and all the activities and other attributes of spirit are the means by which it comes into the consciousness of its essence; i. e., makes itself actually what it is able to become,- *free*.

VIII. The definition of history given in proposition VII., makes it absolutely universal, since it includes all development, natural and spiritual.

Natural History, in the subjective sense, as botany, zoology, physiology, geology, &c., is the investigation and statement of the development of different departments of nature.

Universal History, in the restricted sense, the sense in which the term is popularly used, applies to human history only; i. e., to the exhibition of spirit in the process of working out the knowledge of what it is able to become.

IX. Any *particular history* is the investigation and statement of the progress of the consciousness of freedom in a particular part of the race, on a particular part of the earth, and during a particular period of time.

X. *United States History* is the investigation and statement of the progress made by the people of the United States in the attainment of the consciousness of freedom, from the beginning to the present time, as this progress is manifested in their arts, sciences, inventions, industries, education, government and religion. Or, stated in another way, it is a record of the steps in the development of the fundamental ideas of the government of the United States, and the ideas which it is still seeking to realize, together with the means by which these steps were taken, and by which the progress of the nation in civilization is secured.

Note.—Some of the oriental nations have not attained the knowledge that spirit,—*man as such*,—is free; and because they do not know this, they are not free. They only know that one, the monarch, is free. But on this very account the freedom of that one is only caprice. He is a despot, not a free man. The consciousness of freedom first arose among the Greeks, and to the extent to which they realized this consciousness, they were free; but they, and also the Romans, knew only that *some* are free, not *man as man*. They therefore held slaves; and their whole life, and the maintenance of their splendid liberty was implicated with the institution of slavery; a fact which made that liberty only an accidental, transient, limited growth. The Germanic nations, which include the English-speaking people, under the influence of Christianity, were the first to come into the consciousness that man as man is free,—that it is freedom that constitutes the essence of spirit. These last mentioned nations have so far come into this consciousness, that not one of them now recognizes *property* in man. But this was a growth, a development, a gradual approach toward the ideal through a long series of steps.

The ideal of the race is one with that of the individual. The race may be viewed as "one man who lives always and learns continually." The individual dies, but the race endures.

In the study of history we find the knowledge of this ideal manifesting itself through the language, literature, arts, sciences, industries, laws, insttiutions, and forms of religious worship of the people whose history we study. Indeed, it is through these outward manifestations that we determine to what extent a people has realized freedom. We may say, then, that progress in the consciousness of freedom is fundamental to all other progress.

What is the Object, or End to be Attained in Teaching History?

Some teachers give instruction in history merely because it is placed among the legal branches in the common school curriculum; they have no other end in view than the fulfillment of the letter of the law which requires them to teach it.

Others, perhaps, in addition to the above, have a love for facts and figures, and delight to display their knowledge of them before their classes; and the pupils are encouraged to store their minds with the facts and dates of history that they may have the pleasure of knowing what their teacher knows, of feeling what he feels, and of being able to do what he can do.

Another class teach it for the purpose of holding up before their pupils the failures and successes of past generations, encouraging them to copy the one while they avoid the other.

There is still another class who see that, other things being equal, he is best prepared for the duties and responsibilities of citizenship, who has the profoundest knowledge of the history and principles of the government under which he lives. To this class, therefore, the end or purpose of teaching history is the making of good citizens.

Is there any higher or more comprehensive end than these?

Since history is the record of a development, and a development reveals a plan, and a plan presupposes a planner, the teacher should lead the pupil to see the purposes of the planner revealed, unfolded, bodied forth in the successive steps of the development. The insight, thus gained, into the magnificent plans revealed in universal history will convince him that "what has come to pass, and what is coming to pass every day, is not only not without God, but is essentially his work." * When the plan is comprehended and recognized as God's plan, the result is the justification of God in the history of the universe.

Now, if he be thus led to see that God has an ideal for mankind to realize, viz., freedom, and that the ideal is the same for the individual as for the race, he must see that his own highest good consists in realizing that ideal in himself. He will be led to see that it is not enough that he assert his freedom against irrational and unjust requirements from without, but that he must assert it against caprice, passion, prejudice and sensuality from within. He will be led to recognize, also, that though there are various races of men, there is but one Human Family; that all nations are linked together in one universal Brotherhood; that "Humanity is one vast organism, complex, but still one, throbbing with one life, animated by one soul, every part sympathizing with every other part, and the whole advancing in one indefinite career of progress." † Such a view must lift him out of a narrow selfishness into a broad sympathy, which in its exercise, takes in the whole world. The struggles of any part of the race toward a higher ideal will excite in him the liveliest interest, and

---

* Hegel.   † Sumner.

their successes in any direction of true progress will give him a species of enjoyment incomprehensible to one who cannot see beyond the limits of the selfish man's horizon. With such a spectacle of struggles and triumphs before him he will not be content to remain an idle spectator; he will be impelled to cast in his mite of strength toward the furtherance of the great ends of humanity.

To lead the pupil into that state in which he perceives and does what he ought to do, and does it of his own choice, is to lead him to the realization of the highest freedom. Such is the true end of teaching history. This must be so because it is the end revealed in the nature of the subject. This end must be general because it is found in the nature of universal history; and since it is general, it must include all proper specific ends. Therefore, the teacher who succeeds in securing this general object, will succeed in making good citizens; he will teach moral lessons from the failures and successes of past generations; he may display a wonderful knowledge of facts and dates, and secure the same in his pupils; he will fulfill the letter of the law which requires him to teach history in the common schools, and, what is infinitely better, he will fulfill its spirit.

How teach History? By what Method can the End sought be best secured?

Two elements enter into every rational method of studying or teaching any subject: first, the *plan* embodied in the thing studied; and second, the *laws* of the mind's activity. These two things have been so created as to be exactly adapted to each other. If this were not so, there could be no progress in the development of a single one of the sciences, natural or spiritual. Every subject contains within itself the key to its own method. It follows, then, that the method to be applied to any subject is not something to be made to order, but is to to be found in. and drawn from, the subject itself.

Every subject exists under certain relations. These relations are the conditions under which the mind knows it, and are called the *laws of knowing*. They are, as commonly stated, *Time, Space, Subtance and Attribute, Whole and Part, Likeness and Difference, Cause and Effect, and Design.* These are fundamental ideas, and some of them are necessarily employed in every act of thinking or knowing.

In order, therefore, to perfect our knowledge of anything, i. e., to know that thing fully, and to make it a matter of *permanent* knowledge, we must not only know the fact or facts of its mere existence, but we must know it in all its relations.

The plan of study derived from the foregoing considerations, may be stated as follows :

1. Study the thing in itself,—the facts of its existence,— find its limitations or its attributes, the marks which distinguish it from other things.

2. Fix it in time and space, and in its time and space relations to other things.

3. Study it as a whole composed of related parts; also view each part as a whole composed of parts, when it can be done.

4. Compare and contrast it with other things; i. e., find their likenesses and differences; also compare and contrast the parts with each other.

5. Study it as cause and effect; i. e., viewed as a cause what effects does it produce, and as an effect, what causes produced it ?

6. Study it with reference to design; seek to know the *plan* that it embodies; the purpose for which it exists.

7. Study patiently, persistently, and energetically.

8. Review frequently.

This is no artificial system of mnemonics, nor is it a short cut to the mastery of a subject. It must be perfectly natural, however, because it is grounded in the nature of the mind and of the thing to be known. It calls for close application, patient research, clear, logical thinking, and a determined purpose; and yet it is, in the very nature of things, as short a method as will insure complete, and therefore permanent knowledge.

It is frequently, and too often justly, charged that the instruction given in our common schools is not practical; and particularly is this charge made against the instruction in United States History. Facts out of relation, or facts whose relations are not perceived by their possessor, are of little value. In so far as facts are taught without leading the pupils to see, sooner or later, their relations to some phase of their own lives, just so far the instruction fails. Now, if the teacher in preparing for his work, studies his subjects according to this plan, he will know them in their relations; and when he commences teaching he will see the end from the beginning,—he will know *what* he is to teach, *why* he is to teach it, and *how* he is to teach it. His instruction will be systematic, effective, practical, and enjoyable.

OUTLINE

OF A

COURSE OF STUDY

IN

UNITED STATES HISTORY.

[NOTE.—This outline is intended rather as a guide to teachers in studying the subject for themselves, than in teaching it to beginners. The judgment of the teacher will determine how far it is to be used in the class-room in connection with the text-book.]

DIVISION OF THE SUBJECT INTO RELATED PARTS.

United States History, as a whole, extends in time, from—— (an indefinitely remote period) to the present. Its parts are:

1. The Aboriginal Period,——to 1492.
2. The Period of Discoveries, 1492 to 1607.
3. The Period of Settlements, 1607 to 1689.
4. The Period of Inter-colonial Wars, 1689 to 1763.
5. The Period of the Revolution, 1763 to 1789.
6. The Period of National Development, 1789 to 1861.
7. The Period of the Civil War, 1861 to 1865.
8. The Period of Reconstruction, 1865 to——.

I.

ABORIGINAL PERIOD, ——TO 1492.

1. Why this period is so named, why so bounded in time, and why introduced in the study of U. S. History.

2. Comparison and contrast of North America with South America in respect of position, outline, surface, climate, and productions—mineral, vegetable, and animal.

3. From this comparison and contrast, determine their relative fitness to serve as the physical basis for the development of a highly civilized people.

4. In like manner determine the relative value of British America and the United States; also, of Mexico and the United States.

[NOTE.—This comparison and contrast may be made an excellent review of the Geography of the countries compared and contrasted.]

5. Human inhabitants of America during this period.

a. The Mound Builders.—See Smithsonian Contributions, Vol. I.,—Squier and Davis on "Ancient Monuments;" Baldwin's "Ancient America;" Foster's "Prehistoric Races of America;" Jones' "Mound Builders of Tennessee;" North American Review, Vol. cxxii. pp. 265–308; also, Vol. cxxiii, pp. 60–85; "The Early Man of N. A." in Popular Science Monthly, March, 1877; "Wonders of the Lowlands," Harper's Magazine, February, 1875.

b. The Esquimaux.—See any good Cyclopedia; Dr. Kane's "Arctic Expedition;" "The Cruise of the Florence," in N. A. Review, January, 1879; "The Seven Little Sisters."

c. American Indians.—Good brief sketches in Quackenbos', Seavey's, Goodrich's, and Taylor's Histories of the U. S.; Schoolcraft's "History and Condition of the Indian Tribes;" Cooper's "Leatherstocking Tales;" Introduction to Parkman's "Jesuits in America."

d. Ancient Mexicans or Aztecs.—Their agriculture, manufactures, trade or barter, architecture, education, science, government, and religion.—Prescott's "Conquest of Mexico;" Draper's

" Intellectual Development of Europe;" Baldwin's "Ancient America;" Foster's "Prehistoric Races of America;" N. A. Review, August, 1880, et seq.; Cyclopedias.

e. Ancient Peruvians.—Same topics as above. See Prescott's "Conquest of Peru;" Draper's "Intellectual Development of Europe;" Baldwin's Ancient America;" Foster's " Prehistoric Races of America;" Cyclopedias.

II.
PERIOD OF DISCOVERIES, 1492 to 1607.

1. Historical Conditions in the Old World, preparing for, and making possible the discovery of the New.

a. The Crusades.—See Cyclopedias; any good work on General History; Guizot's "History of Civilization;" Hallam's "Middle Ages;" James' "Chivalry and the Crusades;" "Chronicles of the Crusades;" Walter Scott's " Talisman," and " Betrothed;" Fuller's "Holy War;" Proctor's "History of the Crusades;" Gray's " Children's Crusade;" Goodrich's " History of the Sea."

b. Travels of Marco Polo, Sir John Mandeville, and others, by land, in the East. See Cyclopedias; Harper's "Marco Polo and his Book;" Article on "Geography," Chamber's Cyclopedia; Goodrich's " History of the Sea."

c. Explorations under the direction of Prince Henry, of Portugal. These were by sea, giving a maritime turn to exploration. See Cyclopedias; Irving's " Columbus;" Ladies' Repository, 1869, pp. 333 and 444; Major's "Prince Henry the Navigator;" Goodrich's "History of the Sea."

d. Improvement of the Mariner's Compass.—Its influence in promoting maritime discoveries. See Cyclopedias; " The Sea and its Living Wonders, part III.; Prescott's " Ferdinand and

Isabella;" Irving's "Columbus;" Major's "Prince Henry;" Goodrich's "History of the Sea."

e. Invention of Printing.—See Cyclopedia articles on Printing, Gutenberg, and Coster or Koster; Parley's "Benefactors;" "Printing," in "First Century of the Republic;" same in Harper's Magazine, March, 1875.

f. Beginnings of the Protestant Reformation.—Read sketches of Wickliffe, Huss, Savonarola; Life of Martin Luther; Dew's "Digest of Ancient and Modern History;" Draper's "Intellectual Development of Europe;" Fisher's and D'Aubigne's Histories of the Reformation.

g. The Political Condition of Europe in the 15th Century.—The struggles of the Nations of Western Europe for commercial supremacy, as a means to secure political power, led to rivalries which greatly stimulated maritime enterprise.

2.   The Law of Nations concerning Claims to newly discovered territory, as agreed to by the Christian States of Europe about the close of the 15th Century.

Two points to this law: *First,* Newly discovered territory should belong to the discoverers.

Second, If the Nation originally making the discovery failed for a long time to take possession by actual occupation, other nations might come in.

Modifications.—If the native inhabitants should prove to be Christians, their rights were to be respected; but if they were not Christians, *i. e.,* Roman Catholics, (the Christianity of the time being Roman Catholicism,) they were fair subjects of plunder and conquest, and the exclusive privilege of plundering and conquering them belonged to the discoverers.   See

Hildreth's U. S. History, Vol. I.; also, Seavey's Goodrich's U. S. History, p. 20.

What assumptions underlying this "Law," concerning the relations of Christians to the heathen, and of each to the world?

Why study this "Law" in connection with the Period of Discoveries?

3. Foundation of Claims to Territory in America.

a. *Spanish Claims.*—Construct a table of discoveries, explorations, &c., accomplished by the Spaniards during this period. For material, see any good text-book.

b. *French Claims.*—Construct table.

c. *English Claims.*—Construct table.

Give the boundaries of the claims of each nation at the close of this period. Observe whether these claims have been founded according to the law.

Are there conflicting claims?

III.
PERIOD OF SETTLEMENTS, OR THE CONFIRMATION OF CLAIMS BY FOUNDING COLONIES. 1607—1689.

Note. In the study of this period, the parts are the separate colonies.

GENERAL TOPICS.

1. Royal grants of territory.

2. Settlements made by English, French, and Spanish.

Study carefully each of the English colonies founded during this period, following the method of study laid down in the introduction.

3. Motives of governments, corporations, and individuals in projecting and planting colonies.

4.   The colonial system of the times.

5.   Charters of the English colonies compared and con-trasted.

6.   Character of inhabitants of these colonies, and of their institutions.

7.   Virginia and Massachusetts, as exponents of different political, social, and religious systems, compared and contrasted.   Observe carefully the influence of these two colonies as leaders of public opinion in the subsequent periods.   See Parton's Lecture on "The Pilgrim Fathers as men of Business."

8.   Make like comparisons and contrasts of other colonies.

9.   Kind of government in each colony, both at the beginning and at the close of this period.

10.   Lack of common sympathy among the English colonies to be observed and accounted for.

The best general reference books on this period are Bancroft's, Abbot's, and Hildreth's United States Histories.

IV.
PERIOD OF INTER-COLONIAL WARS, OR QUARRELS OVER CLAIMS.   1689—1763.

Parts of the Period :—

1.   King William's War, 1689–1697.

2.   Queen Anne's War, 1702–1713.

3.   The Spanish War, 1739–1744.

4.   King George's War, 1744–1748.

5.   French and Indian war, 1754–1763.

KING WILLIAM'S WAR.

a. Causes :—

1.   Revocation of the Edict of Nantes, and persecution of the Huguenots by Louis XIV. of France, which caused an

alliance of England with other Protestant Nations against Louis.

2. James II. of England adhered to the "divine right of kings," and the Catholic religion. The English people believed in their right to a voice in the government, and in the Protestant religion. The English revolution of 1688 drove James from the throne. His cause was espoused by Louis of France.

3. Conflicting claims to territory.

b. Events in the Colonies. See any good text-book on United States History.

c. Results :—

1. Persecution of Protestants allayed.

2. William and Mary, the sovereigns chosen by the English Parliament, were confirmed on the throne, and the principle on which they were chosen, acknowledged by France.

3. Territorial boundaries in America unchanged.

4. Unity of sentiment among English colonies promoted.

QUEEN ANNE'S WAR.

a. Causes :—

1. Louis XIV. tried to place upon the throne of England James Francis Edward, son of James II., while the Parliament had chosen Anne.

2. Louis placed his relative, Philip of Anjou, on the throne of Spain in violation of a treaty to which England was a party for the preservation of the balance of power in Europe.

3. Conflicting claims to territory.

b. Events in the Colonies. See text-books.

c. Results :—

1. Plilip confirmed on the throne of Spain.

2. Anne confirmed on the throne of England.

3. England obtained possession of Hudson Bay Territory, Newfoundland, Nova Scotia, I. of St. Christopher, Gibraltar, and I. of Minorca.

4. England obtained from Spain the "Assiento,"—a contract to furnish the Spanish colonies in America 4,800 negro slaves each year for thirty years, and to carry with them 500 tons of "other goods" each year.

5. Colonial unity still further promoted.

SPANISH WAR.

a. Cause:—England's violation of the commercial clause of the Assiento.

b. Events:—See text-books.

c. Results:—Unimportant.

KING GEORGE'S WAR.

a. Causes :

1. England and France took opposite sides in the war of the Austrian Succession.

2. Louis XV. of France tried to place on the English throne, Charles Edward, grand-son of James II.

3. Conflicting claims to territory.

b. Events:—See text-books.

c. Results :—

1. Maria Theresa confirmed on the Austrian Throne.

2. Charles Edward's claims to the English throne abandoned by France.

3. Territorial boundaries unsettled.

4. Colonies learned to take care of themselves, and their common dangers and common interests bound them together.

FRENCH AND INDIAN WAR.

a. Causes:—

1. England and France took opposite sides in the Seven Year's War in Europe.

2. The chief cause of the war in America was conflicting claims to territory. At the same time, England and France were contending for supremacy in India.

b. Events:—See text-books.

c. Results:—

1. This war gave to England all territory east of the Mississippi River, except the I. and city of New Orleans.

2. It determined whether the United States should be English or French, Protestant or Catholic, monarchical or republican.

3. It gave the English colonists an education in warfare that prepared them for the revolutionary struggle.

Results of the Period of Inter-colonial Wars as a whole:

Teacher and pupils think them out from the study of the period.

V.

PERIOD OF THE REVOLUTION, 1763—1789.

Parts :—1. Parliamentary struggle, 1763—1775.

2. Revolutionary War, 1775—1783.

3. Development and adoption of the Constitution, 1783—1789.

PARLIAMENTARY STRUGGLE.

During the Parliamentary Struggle the colonists tried to maintain their rights as Englishmen by parliamentary means.

Special topics to be considered in studying this part of the period:

a. The various oppressive acts of the British Parliament.

b. The Congresses of 1765, 1774, and 1775. What they did. Observe that in 1774 the general government of the colonies was transferred from the British crown to the American Congress by the will of the colonists, and the United States became, in fact, a new nation.

c. Colonial associations formed for opposition to British oppression:

1. Sons and daughters of liberty.
2. Non-importation societies.
3. 'Anti-English luxury societies.

d. Quartering of troops.

e. Tea-tricks of Lord North, and other attempts to bribe the colonists to yield their principles.

f. Committees of correspondence and inquiry appointed to promote the dissemination of news in the colonies, and to secure unity of sentiment and action. (Very important).

g. Organization of colonial militia.

h. Division of the people into two parties,—Whigs and Tories.

i. American lawyers were at this time giving much earnest study to Blackstone's Commentaries on English Law, which had just been published. In the numerous public meetings the masses of the people were instructed concerning their rights under the laws of England.

Thomas Paine's writings, "Common Sense," "The Crisis," and "A Crisis Extraordinary," were powerful appeals in behalf of independence.

j. Statesmen of the Revolution educated for the coming great struggle.

k. Old political ideas cleared up, and more advanced ones developed.

l. Affection of colonies for England supplanted by a desire for independence.

m. Petty strifes between colonies forgotten, and a close union produced.

m. Restrictions of the British Parliament on commerce and manufactures, led the colonists to manufacture at their homes the most necessary articles, and when the war came, they were prepared to provide themselves. Thus England, by her short-sighted policy, educated her colonies for independence.

In this part of the period were clearly developed the causes of the American Revolution. They may be summarized in the following propositions and remarks :

I.   The British government claimed the right to regulate and control the entire trade and commerce of the colonies. This was claimed on the ground that Parliament was the supreme legislature, and had a right to legislate for all parts of the empire, including the colonies. Parliament did exercise this control, as is shown by her various Navigation Acts, and acts imposing duties on imports.

Remarks. At first the colonists scarcely called this right in question, as it was in accordance with the *colonial system* adopted by the European states of the time.

The colonial system was this : that no colony should have any commercial intercourse with other parts of the world, except through the mother country.

The chief advantages of possessing colonies were:

1. That the trade and commerce of the mother country might be enlarged, and her merchants and navigators enriched.

2. That the number of seamen engaged in the merchant service might be increased, from which the government might draw recruits for the navy in time of war.

Any nation depending for its safety on a powerful navy, as was the case with England, encounters great difficulty in obtaining sailors to man the war vessels. There is little difficulty in building and equipping ships, but there is much in obtaining a trained crew, for it takes a long time for one to become a good sailor.

England aspired to rule the ocean, and by her navigation laws she secured both the above named advantages. The colonists submitted at first because their lot was the common lot of all colonies at that time; besides, they were too weak to resist.

II. The British government claimed the right to appoint colonial governors, who should hold office during the king's good pleasure. Besides this, it was claimed that the governors should be made independent of the colonies by a permanent salary, to be paid by the colonists.

Remarks. The colonists wished to make annual grants for the governor's salary, so as to put him under obligation to manage political affairs to please the people, thus making him fear that if he did not do so, the legislature would make trouble about voting his salary. At all events, the principles of his administration would come before the colonial assembly for discussion every year. In England this was considered as subjecting the governor to great indignity, as it tended to make him directly responsible to the people,—an idea wholly at variance with those prevailing in European monarchies at that time concerning the proper relation of ruler and subject.

III. It was claimed by the British Government that all colonial judges should be appointed by the king, and hold office during his good pleasure.

Remarks. The colonists did not object to the king's appointing the judges; but when once appointed they wished to have them made wholly independent by securing them in office during good behavior; because cases would come before the judges in which the rights and privileges of the colonists would come in conflict with the prerogatives of the crown. In such cases there was no security for an impartial decision if at any time the king could remove one judge and appoint another. The colonists claimed that an *independent judiciary* was the only safeguard against the usurpations of governmental power.

IV. The British government claimed the right of direct or internal taxation.

Remarks. The first of the four great matters of difference between the colonies and Great Britain; viz., the right to regulate and control the trade and commerce of the colonies, clearly includes the right of *indirect* taxation, or the levying and collecting duties on imports. It also logically includes the right of *direct* taxation, or the levying and collecting of taxes on each person in the community according to the amount and kind of property which he owns, or the employment he follows, or his income.

Although the British Government claimed both these rights, it had, up to this time, put in practice only the first, for the following reasons:

1. For a long time the population of the colonies was so small and scattering, and the amount of property possessed by the inhabitants was so insignificant that a *direct* tax would have yielded but little revenue, while the expense of collecting it would have been great.

2. The tax on imported goods was easily collected at the ports of entry, and was less obnoxious to the people; hence the government practiced the right of *indirect* taxation at an early period.

3. While the French held possession of Canada and the Mississippi Valley, and the Spanish held Florida, England was somewhat cautious in the treatment of her colonies, for she feared troublesome complications might arise from a serious disagreement between herself and them.

Finally, however, the growing wealth of the colonies, and the increased expenses of the government, growing out of costly wars, led to the exercise of the right of direct taxation.

In addition to this, by the treaty of Paris in 1763, both France and Spain surrendered to England their possessions east of the Mississippi. Now, with Canada in her hands, all the forts manned by British troops, and all the ports filled with British war-vessels, and, having no dangerous neighbors to contend with, the Parliament felt that it had the *power*, as well as the right, to enforce the payment of direct taxes. This it attempted to do by the Stamp Act.

The colonists did not object to paying their share of the expenses of the government, but they claimed that the amount to be assessed, and the manner of its collection, should be determined by their own legislatures.

They grounded this claim on certain inherent and indefeasible rights, vested in every Englishman by the principles of the British Constitution.

The theory of the British Constitution is, that the king has the inherent and indefeasible right to govern the country without any dictation or control of the people; and that it is the inherent and indefeasible right of the people, (meaning by the people, that portion of them represented in the House of Commons) to pay or withhold the expense of his government as they please, without any dictation or control of the king.

This system practically transfers the power to the people, for the king can do nothing without the revenues supplied by his subjects. If his policy be obnoxious to the people, the Parliament has only to withhold the means for executing it, and his policy must fail

Since the colonial legislatures were the only bodies in which the colonists were represented, they claimed that those bodies had the right to determine the whole matter of colonial taxation.

For a fuller statement of the above points, see Abbott's "Revolt of the Colonies;" Bancroft's "History of the United States;" Frothingham's "Rise of the Republic."

REVOLUTIONARY WAR.

Two general classes of topics are to be studied here, political and military.

The principal topics of the first class are:—

a. Foreign relations.

b. Finances of the Revolution.

c. The Declaration of Independence. Study the Declaration itself, and observe that most of the points made in it are found in one or another of the foregoing propositions.

d. Relations of the colonies to one another and to the Congress.

e. The Articles of Confederation.

f. Provisions of treaty at close of war.

Under the military topics should be studied :—

a. The principal campaigns of the war, time and place of each ; parts of each, and the relations of the parts to each other and to the whole; plan and purpose of each; principal battles and their results.

b. Turning point of the war found in the failure of Burgoyne's Campaign. This should be well studied. See Creasey's "Fifteen Decisive Battles."

c. Comparison and contrast of the British and American armies in respect of motives, discipline, equipments and efficiency.

d. Condition and services of the United States navy during the war.

e. Leading officers on both sides.

f. Disbanding of the Army.

General Topics.

a. Meaning of the term "revolution," as applied to a government.

b. Distinction between *revolution, rebellion, insurrection, sedition.*

c. Is a revolution in a government necessarily accompanied by war? Illustrate.

d. What is the difference between the American Revolution and the American Revolutionary War?

e. Which colonies were leaders of public opinion during this time?

f. Boundaries of the United States at the close of the war. Why was the western boundary located as it was?

g. What was accomplished for the rights of mankind, by this war?

General references:—Brancroft; Hildreth; Lossing's Field-Book of the Revolution ; Carrington's Battles of the Revolution ; Biographies of the political and military leaders of the time ; also, works of fiction and poetry pertaining to events of this period.

DEVELOPMENT AND ADOPTION OF THE CONSTITUTION.

a. Removal of motives to union by the close of the Revolutionary War led to looseness in the relation of states to the general government.

b. Defects of Articles of Confederation made a stronger general government necessary.

c. Commercial rivalries led to calls for different conventions to revise the Articles.

d. Inability of general government to collect taxes, to pay debts, or enforce the laws, made the people feel the need of a better constitution.

e. Constitutional convention.

f. Relation of Ordinance of 1787 to Constitution. See N. Review, Vol. cxxii., p. 229; Walkers History of Athens Co., Ohio.

g. Ratification of the Constitution by the people in the separate States.

Note.—Here should follow either the study of the Constitution from a good text book on the subject, or the teacher should present to his class a series of well prepared talks on the subject, in such way as to give his pupils clear ideas of the leading points and principles in it, so that the history following its adoption may be interpreted in the light of the Constitution.

References.—Any good text-book on the Constitution; Story on the Constitution; Elliott's "Debates on the Constitution;" Frothingham's "Rise of the Republic;" Brancroft's "Foot-Prints of time;" "The Federalist."

VI.

PERIOD OF NATIONAL DEVELOPMENT, 1789—1861.

1.　Condition of the United States at beginning of period in respect of population, agriculture, commerce, manufactures, education, religion.

2.　Organization of the government under the Constitution; Election of President and Congress; meeting of Congress; inauguration of President; organization of Executive Departments and appointment of heads; organization of Judiciary and appointment of Judges; Hamilton's financial scheme.

3.　Study of each Presidential administration as a part of the period, following the plan laid down in the introduction.

For a general review of the period the following topics are suggested :

1.,　Viewing the period as a whole, what are its principal parts?　As a part, what is the whole?　Give its time limits.

2.　Name the Presidential administrations of the period, and give the time of each.

3.　What event marks the division between this period and the preceding?　What political parties were formed at this time? What was the immediate question on which the people were divided?

4. Trace the history of political parties through the period.

5. What were the most important questions before Congress at the organization of the government? How was each disposed of?

6. Discuss Hamilton's financial scheme. What points did it comprehend?

7. Connection of the French Revolution with the history of the United States in the first three administrations.

8. Foreign wars of the United States, time, causes, and results of each.

9. Indian wars of this period, time, causes. and results of each.

10. Most important questions at issue in the war of 1812. These were of deep interest to all nations.

They were: *First,* The commercial rights of neutral nations trading with belligerents. *Second,* The right of a citizen of one country to withdraw his allegiance, and become naturalized in another. How these questions were settled.

11. The "Monroe Doctrine," when and why promulgated.

12. The History of the U. S. Bank.

13. History of the great financial crises of the period.

14. Important compromises of this period; time of each, questions at issue, and how settled.

15. Distinction between Mason and Dixon's Line and the Missouri Compromise Line. Location and history of each.

16. Boundary of the U. S. on the S. W. as completed in 1821 by treaty with Spain. This boundary and the Missouri Com-

promise thought in connection with the later political prospects of the North and South.

17.   Connection of the above points with the annexation of Texas, and the Mexican war.

18.   States admitted into the Union during the first forty years of the government; the order of admission observed and accounted for.

19.   Additions of territory made to the U. S. since the organization of the government.   When and by what means each addition was made.

20.   The doctrine of "States Rights," what is meant by it. Occasions upon which this question has been prominently before the people.

21.   Origin and influence of the maxim, "To the victors belong the spoils."

22.   Contrast between the Presidents previous to 1829, and those since.   Causes and results of the difference.

23.   Increase and distribution of population.   Blending of nationalities, benefits and dangers of this.

24.   Influence of separation of Church and State.   Multiplication of religious denominations.

25.   Growth of industries.   Influence of inventions. Some of the most important ones named and their historical importance shown.

26.   Progress in science and popular education.   History of public school system.

27.   Leading statesmen and writers of the period, and the work of each.

28.   Growth of sectional jealousy between North and South. Relation of this to the Civil war.

References.—Works of Adams, Jefferson, Calhoun, Everett, Sumner; Benton's "Thirty Year's View;" Lossing's "Field-Book of the war of 1812;" History of the Mexican War; Wilson's "Rise and Fall of the Slave Power in America;" Harpers' "First Century of the Republic;" Centennial editions of Lossing's, Barnes's, and Ridpath's Histories; Bryant and Gay's "History of United States;" Johnston's "American Politics;" "American Statesman;" Biographies of leading men.

VII.
THE CIVIL WAR, 1861—1865.

1. Its causes found in the preceding period.
2. Its chief campaigns examined.
3. Comparison and contrast of armies.
4. Motives and principles involved.
5. Finances of the Civil war.
6. Foreign relations during this time.
7. Results :—*a.* On the sections—North and South; *b.* On the country as a whole.

References.—Draper's, Greeley's, Stephens', Pollard's, Foote's, Abbott's, Mahan's, Lossing's, and Thayer's Histories of the war; Biographies of the leading men.

VIII.
RECONSTRUCTION OF THE UNION, AND PROBLEMS CONNECTED THEREWITH.

On Reconstruction, there is little in books. Many able articles from both Northern and Southern men have appeared in the N. A. Review and other current magazines.

NOTES

ON THE

CIVILIZATION

OF THE

ANCIENT MEXICANS&PERUVIANS.

MEXICANS.

The ancient history of Mexico embraces two distinct periods: first, from the seventh to the twelfth century, when it was occupied by the Toltecs; second, from the beginning of the thirteenth century to the year 1521, when it was under the dominion of the Aztecs, or Mexicans.

The territory occupied by these peoples embraced but a small part of what is now the Republic of Mexico. It extended, on the Gulf coast, from eighteen degrees to twenty-one degrees north latitude; and on the Pacific coast, from fourteen to nineteen degrees north. These are the limits assigned to it at the time of its conquest by the Spanish in 1521. Although its area is not more than one hundred forty-four thousand square miles, its formation is such as to present a great variety of climate, and at the time of the conquest, was capable of yielding nearly every fruit found between the equator and the Arctic circle.

The Toltecs were a people who had reached a considerable degree of civilization, as is attested by the remains of their architecture, which were found by the Mexicans when they took possession of the territory. It is not certainly known why the Toltecs left the country, but it is said, that having been decimated by famine, pestilence and war, they went southward into Central America, where they are supposed to have produced those wonderful specimens of architecture whose ruins can be seen to-day at Uxmal, Copan, and Palñeque. These ruins, says a recent writer, can be compared only with the ruins of Rome in her glory. The Toltecs were succeeded by the Chichimecs, (or barbarians) who occupied the country about a century, when the Aztecs came in. After living a wandering life for some time, the Aztecs settled at the city of Mexico. It is quite certain that they were not so highly civilized as the Toltecs, and much of the knowledge which they possessed when the Spaniards conquered them, was borrowed from their predecessors. The Aztecs were a conquering people, subjugating the neighboring tribes, or compelling them to pay tribute. Like the Gothic conquerors of Rome, they learned readily the lessons of a higher civilization, and at the time of the Spanish conquest, were, in some respects, the superiors of their conquerors. The principal features of their civilization may be stated under the following heads: Agriculture, Manufactures, Trade or Barter, Architecture, Science, Education, Government and religion.

NOTE. In the preparation of these notes the writer has consulted freely, Prescott's Conquest of Mexico; Foster's Prehistoric Races of America; Baldwin's Ancient America; Drapers Intellectual Development of Europe; various cyclopedias; and a series of articles in the North American Review, so far as they have appeared at the time of writing.

AGRICULTURE.

The agriculture of the Mexicans was superior to that of Europe. They cultivated maize, tobacco, cotton, cacao, maguey, vanilla, and a great variety of fruits. The maguey furnished food, drink, writing material, and roofs for the poorer class of houses. When their soil became exhausted, they restored it by rotation of crops, or by allowing it to lie fallow. The dryness of the soil was relieved by irrigation and by protecting their forests. They built excellent granaries into which they gathered their harvests. Almost all classes engaged in this employment, the women doing the lighter work of the field. As they used no animals of draft, the work was all done by human strength. The wealthy classes, especially the kings and nobles, had gardens stocked with fruits and flowers which for variety and richness were not equaled in Europe. These gardens were scientifically laid out, and the plants were arranged accordingly. In one part there was an aviary stocked with every species of birds known in the realm and noted for beauty of plumage or richness of song. In another part was an aquarium, built of stone and supplied with a great variety of fish. Here and there were artificial fountains sparkling in the the sunlight. There were cascades, and statues, and many other things giving evidence of a degree of culture and a refinement of taste which do not belong to a savage people.

MANUFACTURES.

They manufactured various kinds of cloth from cotton and the fibres of the maguey; leather, and exquisitely beautiful feather goods; a great variety of utensils from gold, silver, copper, clay, and wood; tools, as, hammers, hatchets, chisels, and implements of war from copper, or a bronze of copper and tin. They·made knives, razors, and serrated swords from obsidian, a very hard, dark, transparent mineral, found

abundantly in the mountains of Mexico. They were familiar
with the casting of metals, although, like all the other native
races of America, they knew nothing of the use of iron. Jew-
elry and toys were made in abundance. Some of the silver
vases were so large that a man could not encircle them with
his arms. They imitated very nicely the figures of animals,
and could so skilfully mix the metals that the feathers of a
bird, or the scales of a fish, should be alternately of gold and
silver. A great variety of pottery, for domestic use, and colored in every hue, was made from clay; and the fields are,
to-day, strewn with little figures of idols in every shape made
of the same material. Some of their terra-cotta figures are
genuine works of art. M. Charnay, on the 12th of May, 1880,
made an excavation in the ruins of Teotihuacan, thirty-one
miles northwest of the city of Mexico, from which he made a
collection of one hundred twenty-five heads of idols and
many other objects, among them some perfectly modeled
masks. He says, "Among these Indian masks which appear
to reproduce all the races of Mexico from infancy to old age,
    *   *   *   we find two figures of exceptional interest.
One of these specimens is a negro's head with thick lips and
woolly hair, all perfectly designed; the other, the face of a
woman, rather disfigured by a broken nose, but plainly of
European or Grecian type, and reminding us, by its features,
of the Venus of Milo!" (North American Review, Sept., 1880).

They manufactured dye-stuffs from mineral, vegetable, and
animal material; among them was the rich crimson of the
cochineal. *Pulque*, an intoxicating beverage, of which they
were excessively fond, was made from the fermented juice of
the maguey. The modern Mexican is quite as fond of it as was

his Aztec predecessor. Books, paper, chocolate, medicines and perfumery, were also among their manufactures.

TRADE OR BARTER.

The Aztec merchants did not carry on their business in shops, but at fairs or market-places. They also traveled as itinerant traders, journeying in well armed caravans, going from city to city to attend the fairs, which were held in all the principal towns on the fifth, or last day of the week. These fairs were thronged by a numerous concourse of people, who came to buy or sell from all the neighboring country. A particular part of the market-place was assigned to each article. There were officers in attendance whose duty it was to preserve the peace and prevent frauds. Cheating of all kinds was severely punished. The articles bought and sold were their agricultural products, manufactured articles, and slaves, who were the carriers of the goods. When the slaves were exposed for sale they were dressed in their gayest clothing, and instructed· to sing, dance, and display their little stock of personal accomplishments, so as to recommend themselves to the purchaser. The slave-trade, among the Aztecs, was as honorable as it was among their Spanish conquerors. Traffic was carried on partly by barter, and partly by means of a sort of currency. This consisted of transparent quills of gold dust; of bits of tin and of copper, cut in the form of a **T**; and of bags of cacao, consisting of a specified number of grains. The calling of the merchant was considered a very honorable one, and was frequently the stepping-stone to high political position.

ARCHITECTURE.

Their houses were built of stone, of sun-dried brick, or of

clay. Some of the buildings, especially the temples and palaces, were coated with cement which was overlaid with white stucco very highly polished. The streets in the towns were paved either with stone or with colored and polished cement, and were kept very clean. In the ruins of some of the ancient cities portions of the streets are still found covered with this cement. The roofs of the poorer class of houses were thatched with palm leaves or a preparation from the maguey ; of the better classes, the roofs were flat or terraced. Cedar and other aromatic and ornamental woods were used for ceiling and for various kinds of fancy finishing.

The residences of the nobles were artistically arranged, many of them covering vast areas of ground and enclosing an open court. Very often the sides were set off by marble porticoes, and the corners ornamented by sculptured stone-work.

The descriptions given of the royal palaces remind one of the accounts given of Solomon's temple. If they were at all like the descriptions, they were wonderful. In the construction of one of these palaces, two hundred thousand men are said to have been employed. It was decorated with beautifully wrought silver and gold, artistically carved wood, and magnificent tapestry of feather-work. In this building there were the council chamber and halls of justice, accommodations for foreign ambassadors, and spacious apartments for men of science and letters, whom the monarch invited to his court. The dwellings were usually low, seldom being more than one story in height. The doors had no shutters, but instead, there were suspended in the door-ways, mats bordered by ornaments of copper or other metal, whose tinkling would announce the coming of the visitor.

Their temples were built of sculptured stone, often reaching many stories in height and surmounted by a dome of polished black marble, studded with stars of gold in imitation of the sky. These temples frequently rested on pyramids of great size. One of these, called the Pyramid of the the Sun, now standing at the ruined city of Teotihuacan, has a base seven hundred sixty-one feet square, and a height of two hundred sixteen feet. Charnay says it exactly faces the four cardinal points.

They built strong fortresses of stone, frequently surrounding the fort proper, as well as their cities, with high walls.

Excellent bridges were common, and many of them could be drawn or raised. Fine aqueducts were built for the purpose of conveying water from distant springs into the cities.

On the whole, their architecture had not the lightness and airiness of that of the Spaniards, yet, it was solid, and at the same time was not destitute of beauty.

SCIENCE.

Astronomy.—They had ascertained the globular form of the earth, and the obliquity of the ecliptic. They knew the cause of eclipses, had ascertained the period of the solstices and equinoxes, and had made sun-dials for determining the hour of the day. At the time of their conquest they had a calendar that was more perfect in its adjustment of civil to solar time than any other known, since more than five centuries must pass, before the loss of a single day would occur.

The year was divided into eighteen months of twenty days each, five complementary days being added each year to make up the three hundred sixty-five days. These five days did not belong to any month, and were considered as being peculiarly unlucky. To provide for the six additional hours of the year they added twelve and a half days every fifty-two years. The month was divided into four weeks of five days each, the last of which was the day of the public fair or market. The day was divided into sixteen hours, beginning at sunrise.

NOTE.—A large stone, about eight feet in diameter, twenty-seven feet in circumference, and thirty-three inches in height, was digged up in the great square of the city of Mexico in 1790. In the top of it is a circular depression or cup, eighteen inches in diameter and six inches deep which communicates with a channel terminating in the circumference. The edge is covered with groups of sculptured images. At first this stone was supposed to be connected with the astronomical science of the Aztecs, and it was named the sun-stone or the calendar; but later, other interpretations have been put upon it. For a statement of the different views concerning it, see M. Charnay's article in the North American Review, September, 1880. For a fine representation of it, see the number for October, 1880.

Arithmetic.—They had a system of written as well as of oral arithmetic. The first twenty numbers were expressed by a corresponding number of dots. The first five had specific names; after which up to ten, they were represented by combining the representative of five with that of one of the preceding numbers. Thus, five and one for six, (⋯⋯) five and two for seven, (⋯⋯) and so on. Ten was viewed as two fives, fifteen as three fives, twenty as four fives, and each received a separate name. Ten was represented by two rows of five dots each, fifteen by three rows, and twenty by four. Twenty was also expressed by a separate hieroglyphical symbol, a flag. Larger sums were reckoned by twenties, and were represented by repeating the number of flags. The square of twenty, four hundred, had a separate sign, a plume, and so had the cube of twenty, or eight thousand, which was represented by a purse, or sack. For greater expedition, they denoted fractions of the larger sums by drawing only a part of the object. Thus half or three-fourths of a plume or purse represented that portion of the sums denoted by those objects. This is said to be the whole of their arithmetical system of notation, by the use of which they were enabled to indicate any integral quantity.

Botany.—They knew something of botany as was shown by the scientific arrangement of their gardens, though they had not made the progress in this science that they had in astronomy and mathematics.

Medicine.—Perhaps no country in the world affords a greater variety of medicinal plants than Mexico, and their virtues were well known to the Mexican physicians who are said to have studied medical botany as a science.

History and Chronology ranked as sciences among them, and persons were especially trained for keeping the records of time and events. These records were kept by a kind of hieroglyphics, or picture writing.

All their scientific works, astronomical, chronological, historical, &c., were submitted to the judgment of a Council of Music, as it was called, before they could be made public.

EDUCATION.

The education of the youth was monopolized by the priesthood, thus keeping society within their control. There were buildings erected within the enclosures of the temples, for the special purposes of education. Here the children of both sexes of the upper and middle classes were placed at an early age. The girls were entrusted to the care of priestesses, from whom they learned various feminine employments, especially the weaving and embroidering of rich coverings for the altars of the gods. They were also instructed in music and the songs of the bards.

The boys were drilled in the performance of certain rites and ceremonies connected with their religion. In the higher schools they were initiated into the mysteries of hieroglyphics, were taught their traditionary history, the principles of government, and such branches of science as were within the knowledge of the priesthood.

Great attention was paid to the moral discipline of both sexes. The most perfect order prevailed, and offences were punished with the utmost rigor, sometimes with death itself.

At a suitable age for marrying, or for entering the world the pupils were dismissed from the convent, as it may be called, and those who were most competent received such recommendations as often introduced them to responsible situations in public life.

The council of music, already referred to, decided on the qualifications of the instructors in the various branches of science, and examined the pupils to determine whether or not they had been well taught; if not, it had the authority to punish the instructors. This council seems to have been a general board of education for the whole country. On stated days its members sat in judgment on the merits of historical compositions, and poems treating of moral and traditional topics recited by their authors. On these occasions the monarchs and a large concourse of interested spectators were present to enjoy the recitations. Prizes were distributed to the successful competitors. In this way advancement in science and literature was secured, and a taste was cultivated in the people, which found its gratification in intellectual pleasures.

GOVERNMENT.

The legislative authority was vested in the monarch,

though he himself was subject to the laws of the realm. He was also chief executive, but the burdens of government were distributed among a number of departments; viz., the Council of State, Council of War, Council of Justice, Council of Finance, and Council of Music or Education.

The council of state was the king's cabinet of immediate advisers. The laws were reduced to writing, and were rigidly enforced. The government mandates and public intelligence were transmitted by a well organized postal service of couriers. Post-houses were established on all the great roads, about six miles apart. Each courier ran at the top of his speed from his own station to the next, where he transmitted his news or package to another, who, in turn, carried it to the third. In this way a distance of two hundred miles a day was frequently made. It was no unusual thing for the monarch to eat fish for his breakfast which had been taken the previous morning from the Gulf of Mexico, two hundred miles distant from the capital.

Marriage was regarded as an important social engagement, and was celebrated with as much ceremony as in any Christian country. The marriage relation was held so sacred that a special tribunal was instituted to determine questions pertaining to it, and divorces could not be obtained except with great difficulty, and after a patient hearing of the parties before this court. Polygamy was practiced, but most commonly by the upper classes.

Slavery was recognized in the case of prisoners of war, criminals, and debtors. The slave, however, was allowed to have his own family, to hold property, and even other slaves, but his children were free. No one could be born a slave in Mexico, a provision found in no other country of the world where slavery has been recognized.

The council of war had general charge of the military affairs of the realm. The profession of arms was the recognized vocation of the nobles. The armies, whether in service in the field, or in garrisons, were supported by taxation on the products of the soil and on manufactures. The armies were divided into corps of ten thousand each, and these again into regiments of four hundred. Standards and banners were used, the troops marched to military music, and were provided with hospitals, army surgeons, and a medical staff.

The council of justice was the supreme court of the country. The judges were appointed by the monarch, but he could not remove them at will. They received appeals from lower tribunals, both in civil and criminal cases, and their decision was final.

The council of finance had general charge of the collection and care of the public revenues. These were derived chiefly from taxes on agricultural and manufactured products. Tax-gatherers were distributed throughout the kingdom, and were exceedingly rigorous in their exactions. Every defaulter was liable to be sold as a slave.

The taxes were not paid in money, but in a portion of the articles produced. A receiver-general was stationed at the capital, who received and stored in the public granaries, the contributions as they came in. He had a map of the whole empire, and with it minute specifications of the taxes assessed on every part. These taxes were light at first, but at the coming of the Spaniards they were very oppressive, which led some of the provinces to join Cortez against the

king, thus making the conquest much easier. The duties
of the council of music have already been discussed under
education.

Their Creed.—They all recognized the existence of one supreme Creator and Lord of the universe.

The higher classes were strictly unitarian, acknowledging
but one divinity, and he almighty, invisible, and unrepresentable. They taught their children not to confide in idols,
but only to conform to their worship in deference to public
opinion. They were exhorted to "aspire to that heaven where
all is eternal and where corruption never comes."

The lower classes believed that the behests of the one
supreme deity were executed by a host of inferior ones, to
each of whom some special day or appropriate festival was
consecrated. They worshiped more than two hundred inferior
divinities.

At the head of all these inferior divinities was the war-god.

This was the patron god of the nation. His temples were
the most stately and august of all the public edifices. His
fantastic image was loaded with costly ornaments, and his
altars recked with the blood of human sacrifices in every
town of the empire.

Next to the war-god was the god of the air who had once
dwelt among them and instructed them in the use of metals,
in agriculture, and in the art of government. From some
cause he was driven from the country by a superior deity.
He departed to the east across the Gulf of Mexico. As he
was leaving he told his followers that he would again visit
them. He was described as a tall personage with a white

skin, long dark hair, and a flowing beard. The Mexicans confidently expected his return at about the time the Spaniards made their appearance. Cortez early learned this tradition and announced that he had been sent by their long looked-for deity.

They believed in a future state of existence in which rewards and punishments were to be meted out. They imagined three separate states in the future life; first, a hell of darkness for the wicked, which class, according to their belief, comprehends the greater part of mankind; second, a negative existence of indolent contentment for those who died of certain peculiar diseases; third, a paradise of joy for the heroes who fell in battle, or volunteered to offer themselves as sacrifices to the gods.

It was one of their doctrines that men do not sin of their own free will, but because of the planetary influences under which they are born.

Rites and Ceremonies.—These rites were administered and the ceremonies performed by a very numerous priest-hood whose power exceeded that attained by the Roman Catholic priest-hood. This is shown by the fact that absolution by the priest for civil offences was an acquittal in the eye of the law.

At the birth of a child, the rite of baptism was administered by the priests. They had monastic institutions, the inmates of which prayed three times a day. They practiced ablutions, vigils, and penance by flagellations or by pricking with thorns. They compelled the people to confession, required of them penance, and gave absolution. Confession was performed but once during life, the rich, sacrificing at that time,

numerous slaves as propitiation for their sins. At the death
of an individual imposing burial rites were administered,
prominent among which, if he were rich, was the offering of
great numbers of his slaves, frequently one hundred, as sacrifice to the gods. At the dedication of their temples, thousands of prisoners of war were offered up. The victims were
taken to the top of the temple, where, in the presence of
the multitude of spectators, they were placed one by one on
the convex surface of the stone or sacrifice, which stood in
front of the recess occupied by the idol. Five priests held the
victim on the stone in such a way that his breast was heaved
upward. The chief priest then laid open the breast, and
quickly plucked out the heart, which he held up toward the
sun as an offering; then turning to the idol he threw the
heart at its feet. The bodies were immediately cast down the
stairway, where those who had made them prisoners seized
them, carried them off, divided them among themselves, and
feasted on them with great ceremony.

In these degrading performances we see the greatest hind-
rance to their progress in civilization. But revolting as these
cruelties are, and opposed as they are to the true spirit of civilization, still in some of the most polished countries of Europe after the establishment of the inquisition, there were
tens of thousands of human victims slaughtered in the name,
but surely not in the spirit, of the Christian religion. It becomes us, therefore, to think charitably of the religion of the
Ancient Mexicans.

THE PERUVIANS.

At the time of the Spanish invasion the Empire of Peru extended along the Pacific coast of South America, from about two degrees of north latitude, to about thirty-seven south. Its extent from east to west is not so well known, though it probably did not extend much beyond the Andes to the east. The country, therefore, consisted principally of the great table land of the Andes, a portion of the eastern slope, the western slope, and the narrow strip between the foot of the mountains and the Pacific. The summits of the mountains are covered with eternal snow which extracts the moisture from the eastern winds, giving to the eastern slope a copious rain-fall, while the other portions of the country are left very dry. Notwithstanding this, the principal part of the population was found to the west of the eastern slope.

The civilization of these people will be treated under the same topics that were used in treating of the Mexicans. The same authorities have been consulted, excepting the North American Review.

AGRICULTURE.

The dry slope of the Andes, under the careful culture of the Ancient Peruvians, became one vast garden, immense terraces having been made wherever necessary, and irrigation carried on by canals and aqueducts constructed on a scale unequaled by any other people in the world. Advantage was taken of the different mean annual temperatures of different altitudes to pursue the cultivation of products requiring a great variety of climate. In this pursuit they excelled the Mexicans, following it even more scientifically than they. All classes engaged in it. The monarch, on the occasion of one of their great annual festivals, set the example in the presence of all the people by turning up the earth with a golden plough.

The great canals and aqueducts were built at the public expense. They were constructed of large slabs of stone, nicely fitted together, and, by means of side-drains, they moistened the lands of the lower levels through which they passed. One of these water-ways was between four hundred and five hundred miles long. In some places it was cut through solid rock, in others, conducted around mountains, and in still others, carried across streams, marshes, and mighty chasms. These works were superintended by overseers appointed by the monarch, and their duty was to attend to the distribution of the water along the route, the law prescribing how much should be drawn to the land of each person.

NOTE.—Dr. Steere of Michigan University, who has traveled quite extensively in South America, told the writer a few years ago, that he had seen portions of this great aqueduct in a very perfect state of preservation, and doing duty just as it did probably five hundred years ago, though not in the hands of so skillful agriculturists as it was then.

In order to utilize the sides of the mountains, great terraces were cut, the lower ones containing hundreds of acres; the upper ones wide enough to contain only a few rows of corn. Many of these shelves were so stony that earth had to be spread upon them before they could be cultivated. Fertilizers were abundantly used, especially guano. This was, as it is still, found in immense quantities on many of the little islands along the coast. The islands were assigned by law to the different districts which lay adjacent to them, and all encroachment on the rights of another was severely punished.

The guano-producing birds were protected by law, and the

killing of one of them was punished with death. As another means of fertilizing the ground, in some places, a few little fishes were planted in the hills of corn or other grain.

The plow used by them was generally a strong, sharp pointed stake, with a cross-piece about twelve inches from the point. On this cross-piece the plowman placed his foot to force it into the ground. Having no animals of draft, the plow was drawn by six or eight strong men, who kept time as they moved, by chanting their national songs, in which they were accompanied by the women, who followed, breaking up the clods with their rakes.

They cultivated the banana, cassava, maize, maguey, quinoa, (a small grain resembling rice) tobacco, cinchona, and the tuber mis-named the Irish potato.

The gardens of the nobles and kings, or Incas, were arranged with even greater splendor than those of the Mexicans.

ARCHITECTURE.

Their buildings were made principally of stone or brick. The bricks were made of a tough kind of clay mixed with straw. This mixture was made into large square blocks, much larger than our bricks. The walls were very thick, but low, seldom more than twelve or fourteen feet high, a two story house being a very rare thing. This fact is due to the prevalence of earthquakes. The Spaniards built tall edifices, many of which have been totally demolished, while some of the low, thick walls of the Incas remain to this day. The roofs were usually of straw or wood; though some on the smaller houses were of a singular bell-shape, and made of a composition of cement and pebbles. The doors were the only openings for the admission of light. These were like

the Egyptian doors, narrower at the top than at the bottom.
The rooms had no communication with one another, but
usually opened into a court. The stones of their buildings
were usually rough, except at the joints, where they were made
to fit with the utmost precision. They did not mortise their
timbers together, and being ignorant of iron, they knew no better way of joining them than by tying them with cords of
the maguey. There were many other incongruities in their
houses; for example, the building that was thatched with
straw, and destitute of windows, glowed within with tapes-
tries of gold and silver. The exterior of their buildings was
destitute of that ornamentation which characterized the
architecture of the Mexicans.

Their temples were very numerous but not tall. The
greatest of them was at Cuzco, the capital. It consisted of a
principal building and several chapels and inferior edifices,
covering a large area. It was in the heart of the city, and
was enclosed by a wall, which, like the buildings, was of stone.
The interior was literally a mine of gold. On the western
wall, directly opposite the great eastern door, was a representation of the sun, their great deity, consisting of a human
countenance looking forth from amidst innumerable rays of
light. This figure was engraved on a massive plate of gold
of enormous size thickly powdered with emeralds and other
precious stones. As the rays of the rising sun streamed through
the great eastern door, they fell upon this image lighting up
the whole apartment with a wonderful effulgence which was
reflected and re-reflected by the golden ornaments with
which the walls and ceiling were everywhere studded.

One of the adjacent chapels was dedicated to the moon,

and contained a silver image of that object, made in the same way as that of the sun. All the decorations in this chapel were of silver. Another was dedicated to the stars, another to thunder and lightning, and yet another, to the rainbow, whose many colored arch spanned the walls with hues almost as radiant as those of Iris herself. Every ornament, vase, or vessel; every imitation of flowers, fruits, or animals; every tool, even, for the cultivation of the gardens, belonging to the temples was of gold or silver.

In and around Cuzco there were no less than four hundred places of worship, which were cared for by a very numerous retinue of priests and attendants, the number at the great temple alone, being four thousand.

They built wonderful roads in every direction from the capital. Two extended from Cuzco to Quito, one on the plateau, the other along the coast. They were twenty feet wide, and were paved with flag-stones, or Macadamized with a substance as hard, and almost as smooth as marble. No obstacles were too great to be overcome. The road on the plateau was cut, in some places for miles, through solid rock; hideous ravines were filled up with solid masonry; precipices were scaled by stairways hewn out of the rock; rivers were crossed by bridges suspended in the air, or where such bridges could not be made, they were crossed by ferry-boats or rafts on which sails were used.

The coast road was protected by a wall on either side, and rows of sweet scented shrubbery and shade trees were planted on the border. On all the great roads stones were set up after the manner of mile stones.

Post-houses were built about five miles apart, and twelve

miles apart were great caravansaries or inns for the accom-
modation of the Inca or his troops. Almost all the travel
was for the purposes of the government.

MANUFACTURES.

Many of their manufactures were quite similar to those of
the Mexicans. Besides those, they made a coarse kind of cloth
from the wool of the *llama* and the *alpaca*; and a very fine,
almost silky article, was made from the wool of the *huanaco*
and the *vicuna*, two species of wild sheep inhabiting the
mountain districts. This wool was obtained in the following
manner: every year great hunts were organized in which
thousands of men engaged. They were armed with poles
and spears, and so distributed as to form a circle of immense
extent that should embrace the whole country to be hunted
over. All kinds of game were driven toward the center of the
circle. The beasts of prey were slain without mercy, and the
others, consisting chiefly of deer, the huanacos, and the
vicunas, were not molested until they were concentrated upon
some convenient plain. The male deer, and some of the
coarser kinds of sheep were slaughtered. Their skins were
saved for leather, and their flesh was distributed among the
people, who dried it and ate it. This was the only animal
food eaten by the lower classes of Peru. The fine-wooled
sheep, however, were caught, carefully sheared, and then
allowed to escape. The wool thus obtained was taken to
government store houses, where it was given out to the
most skillful workmen to be made into cloth for the kings
and the nobility.   •

These hunts were not repeated in the same district oftener
than once in four years

From corn, a kind of liquor was manufactured, of which the people were very fond, and of which they often drank to excess.

Every man in Peru was expected to be familiar with the manufacture of all those articles most essential to the household, but there were certain ones who were specially trained to those occupations which furnished articles of luxury to the higher classes of society. These special callings, like all the professions and offices in Peru, descended from father to son. Hence, while there was little originality or boldness of design in their work, there was much skill in execution.

Like the Mexicans, the Peruvians made tools of a bronze of copper and tin. The qualities and characteristics of this substance, found in these widely distant regions, are almost exactly identical. In color it resembles gold; its specific gravity is a little less than 9.; it is malleable, but breaks under sudden and strong bending or twisting; the proportions of the two metals range from about .90 copper with .10 tin, to .98 copper with .02 tin. Many specimens have been chemically analyzed, all giving results about as above stated.

It seems strange that the Mexicans and Peruvians should have no knowledge of each other, and yet do the same thing in the same way.

Although modern science can exactly determine these proportions by analysis, it has not yet succeeded in combining them to produce a bronze possessing exactly the same characteristics.

TRADE OR BARTER.

The Peruvians had no kind of money or other general medium of exchange as the Mexicans had, but they bartered their manufactured and agricultural products at fairs which occurred three times a month. They had scales for determining the quantity of articles, while among the Mexicans, nothing of the kind was found.

SCIENCE.

In astronomy they were far inferior to the Mexicans. The equinoxes and solstices were determined, however; their year ending at the winter solstice. Their calendar was imperfect. They had not those accurate divisions of time used by the Mexicans, and did not know the cause of eclipses.

They had no science of mathematics, their mathematical calculations being made with knotted strings called *quipus*. By combinations of these they represented any required number, but only those who were specially trained to their use, could interpret them.

There was among them no such thing as medical or botanical science. Their medicine man was little more than a conjurer.

EDUCATION.

"Science was not intended for the people, but for those of generous blood. Persons of low degree are only puffed up by it, and rendered vain and arrogant. Neither should such meddle with the affairs of government; for this would bring high offices into disrepute, and cause detriment to the state." This is given by Prescott as a favorite maxim of Tupac Inca Yupanqui, one of the most famous of the Peruvian sovereigns. It furnishes the key to the educational system of Peru, as it does, indeed, to the whole system of government.

As might be expected from the above, education was confined entirely to the nobility. The young nobles were instructed in such matters as would concern them in after life.

They studied the laws and principles of their government, the rites of their religion, the correct use of their own language, the chronicles of the deeds of their ancestors, and the use of the quipus, or knotted strings, by means of which their records were kept. They had no books or paper, and no kind of writing. In their schools, instruction was given by lectures or conversation. The events of their history were largely transmitted by tradition, or by the ballads of their minstrels.

GOVERNMENT.

Their government was one of the most perfect absolutism ever known. The monarch was both law-giver and the law. Any violation of his ordinance was sacrilege, for he was regarded as a divine being, inasmuch as he was descended from the great divinity, the sun.

Society was divided into castes, the limits of which could never be overstepped.

The Incas and nobles practiced polygamy, but the lower castes were limited to one partner each. On a certain day each year, all the young persons of marriageable age,—men twenty-four, women eighteen or twenty—came together in the great squares of the towns all over the empire. The magistrate took the hands of those couples to be united, placed them within each other, and pronounced the parties man and wife. There was little freedom in the choice of partners; indeed it may almost be said that the government made all the matches. A house and a piece of ground were provided for each pair at the expense of the government, and at the birth of each child a little more ground was added. Festivities followed the marriage ceremony, and for a few days, since

the weddings all took place on the same day, there was one
universal bridal jubilee throughout the empire.

The Peruvian army was managed in much the same way
as that of the Mexicans.

In Peru there was no personal freedom. Everything was
under the eye of the government. The individual was de-
pendent for everything. No one was allowed even to be
happy in his own way, for all his enjoyments were prescribed
by law. The government of the Incas was the mildest, but
the most searching of despotisms.

RELIGION.

In their religion we find much less that is revolting than in
that of the Mexicans. The most enlightened believed in an
invisible, unrepresentable Deity, but the masses of the people
worshiped the sun as their god. They believed in the eternal
life of the soul, and in the resurrection of the body. Like the
Egyptians, they embalmed the dead that the bodies might
be preserved for the soul on its return. Their sacrifices were
principally the fruits of the ground. Human sacrifices were
seldom offered except on the occasion of the birth of a royal
heir, a coronation, a great victory, or the death of an Inca.
On these occasions the victim was a little child or a beautiful
maiden. These solemnities were not followed by cannibal
orgies, as was the case in Mexico. They had many religious
festivals, the greatest of which was in honor of the sun, and
lasted three days, terminating with the favorite amusements
of the Peruvians, music, dancing, and drinking.

CONCLUSION.

A comparison of the Mexican with the Peruvian civilization will show that in agriculture and some of the mechanic

arts, Peru was superior; in literature and science, Mexico had reached a higher place; in the consolidation of government and in the certainty of its action Peru was ahead; but in personal independence and freedom of thought and action Mexico was in advance. In their religious systems we find much less that was revolting and cruel among the Peruvians. It is to be regretted that we do not have the means of tracing the steps in the growth of their civilization from their own records, but when these countries were conquered by the Spanish,—Mexico in 1519—1521, by Cortez; Peru in 1531—1532, by Pizarro,—everything of the nature of books or records was destroyed that the Spanish priests could secure. In the towns of Mexico great heaps of manuscripts were collected and burned as "works of the devil." These books represented the labors of many a Mexican poet, historian, and scientist. All that is known of their history previous to the conquest, has been gleaned from stray works that escaped the fanaticism of the bigoted Spaniards, or from the vague traditions of the conquered people.

'Mexico and Peru would have been vastly different to-day if the Spaniards had been sufficiently controlled by Christianity and civilization to treat the people justly, and to seek nothing more than honorable and friendly intercourse with them. At no time since the Spanish conquest has either country been as orderly, as prosperous or as populous as they found it. Industry and thrift have been supplanted by laziness and beggarly poverty."

Draper says. "The enormous crime of Spain in destroying this civilization has never yet been appreciated in Europe. After an attentive consideration of the facts in the case, I

agree in the conclusion of Carli that at the time of the conquest the moral man in Peru, was superior to the European,
and I will add, the intellectual man also. In Spain, or even
in all Europe, was there to be found a political system carried out into the practical details of actual life, and expressed
in great public works as its outward, visible, and enduring
sign, which could at all compare with that of Peru? Its only
competitor was the Italian system, but that for a long time
had been actively used to repress the intellectual advancement of man. In vain the Spaniards excuse their
atrocities on the plea that a nation like the Mexican, which
permitted cannibalism, should not be regarded as having
emerged from the barbarous state, and that one which, like
Peru, sacrificed human hecatombs at the funeral solemnities of great men, must have been savage. Let it be remembered that there is no civilized nation whose popular practices do not lag behind its intelligence; let it be remembered
that in this respect Spain herself also was guilty. In America,
human sacrifice was part of a religious solemnity, unstained
by passion. The burning of Jews and heretics in Europe
was a dreadful cruelty; not an offering to heaven, but a gratification of spite, hatred, fear, vengeance—the most malignant
passions of earth. There was no spectacle on the American
continent at which a just man might so deeply blush for his
race as that presented in Western Europe when the heretic
from whom confession had been wrung by torture, passed to
his stake in a sleeveless garment, with flames of fire and effi-
gies of an abominable import depicted upon it. Let it be
remembered that by the inquisition, from 1481 to 1808, three
hundred forty thousand persons were punished. and of these

nearly thirty-two thousand were burnt.   Let it be also remembered that, considering the worthlessness of the body of man, and that, at the best, it is at last food for the worm—considering the infinite value of his immortal soul, for the redemption of which the agony and death of the Son of God were not too great a price to pay—indignities offered to the body are less wicked than indignities offered to the soul.   It would be well for him who comes forward as an accuser of Mexico and Peru in their sin, to dispose of the fact that at that period the entire authorty of Europe was directed to the perversion, and even total repression of thought—to an enslaving of the mind, and making that noblest creation of Heaven a worthless machine.   To taste of human flesh is less criminal in the eye of God than to stifle human thought."

Theories Concerning Their Origin.

The origin of these peoples and their civilization, is a topic that has been the subject of the most absurd and fanciful speculation, as well as of deep scientific and philosophical research.   The theories advanced are almost as numerous as the men who have studied the subject.   Like most nations whose civilization reaches back of their records, both the Mexicans and the Peruvians had their myths and traditions concerning their origin.   For these, the reader is referred to Prescott's works.

The following are some of the theories that have been promulgated by different writers on the subject:

1.   *The Lost Ten Tribes of Israel.*   The Spanish priests very early devised the theory that the civilization of these people was of Jewish origin.   The ground of the theory was, the many (imagined) resemblances between their religious rituals, the

similarity of architecture, and the use of the cross as a symbol. According to this monkish story these tribes left Palestine, traversed the whole extent of Asia, crossed over into America at Behring's strait, went down the Pacific coast, and established a wonderful civilization in that part of the continent where the great ruins are found. This theory does not receive credence from the learned of our own time.

2. *The "Atlantis" Theory.* This theory supposes that where the central bed of the Atlantic Ocean now is, there was in the remote past a great peninsula, or island, perhaps, of the Western Continent projecting far toward Europe and Africa; that the West Indies and the Azores are the mountains of that region which by some great convulsion of nature was submerged; and that in the great fertile plain lying between the islands mentioned arose the first civilization of mankind, which extended westward to the present America, and eastward to Egypt. In the writings of Plato reference is made to the Atlantes, a powerful people, who, under their three kings, ruled Atlantis, several other islands, and some parts of the continent. Solon learned the account of the island and its submergence, from the Egyptian priests. Many other writers of antiquity mention a great continent or island called Atlantis, lying to the westward of the Old World, and assert that its people and those of Europe had intercourse with each other. Brasseur de Bourbourg, who is the great advocate of this theory, claims that in the New world he finds both traditions and records similar in import to those of the Greeks and Egyptians.

3. *The Malay Theory.* There is some plausibility in the supposition that the Malays brought civilization to this

country. Malay dialects are spoken in many of the Pacific Islands reaching as far eastward as Easter Island which is in the same longitude as the western part of Mexico, and the same latitude as the southern part of the Ancient Peruvian Empire. Traditions in both Mexico and Peru say that their coasts were visited by a foreign people who came from the west in ships. There are many great architectural remains in the Malay archipelago giving evidence of a degree of civilization which, situated as it was, must pre-suppose a knowledge of navigation. The languages of Mexico and Peru, as well as the architectural remains, have nothing in common with those of Malaysia, to warrant the assumption that the civilization of one was derived from the other.

4. *The Phœnician Theory.* Of all the theories supposing the civilization of the New World to have been derived from the old, this is probably the most plausible. The Phœnicians were the greatest maritime adventurers of ancient times. They colonized all shores of the Mediterranean, circumnavigated Africa, and pushed far into the Atlantic beyond the straits of Gibraltar. They penetrated every known sea, and traded on every known coast. It is thought by some that the frequent reference by the ancients to a great continent beyond the Atlantic, must have come through a knowledge of it obtained from the Phœnicians. Since they were such great traders and colonizers it is not difficult to conceive that they may have planted colonies here. Traditions of the Mexicans and Central Americans say their first civilizers were bearded white men who came from the east in ships. The same arguments may be urged against this as against the Malay theory.

5. *The Mound Builder Theory.* By some it is thought that the Mound Builders, were driven from the Mississippi Valley to the southward, where they developed the civilization found there by the European discoverers. Others reverse the theory, and say that the civilization of the Mound Builders came from the south.

6. *The Mongolian Theory.* This theory supposes that the Mongols, or a kindred people, crossed Behrings' strait, wandered to the southward and settled in the valleys of Mexico and the country further to the south.

7. *The Autochthonic Theory.* According to this hypothesis the people found here were created here, and developed their civilization originally. This is the the theory of many able scientists. It was held by Prof. Agassiz, in accordance with his doctrine of "multiple centres of creation."

The investigations of archæologists are leading them to assign to the origin of civilization, not only in America, but in the Old World, a much greater antiquity than was formerly accepted.

PREPARATION

FOR THE

DISCOVERY OF AMERICA.

NOTE. In the preparation of the following matter, the writer has had access to most of the works referred to on pages 17 and 18 of the Outline. He does not claim originality except in the concatenation of the events, and in the idea that these events are parts of a great plan, each of which prepared for another until they culminated in the great event which forms the central thought of the present section of this little book.

The discovery of America by Columbus stands out in history as an event of supreme importance, both because of its value in itself, and because of its reflex action upon Europe. It swept away the hideous monsters and frightful apparitions with which a superstitious imagination had peopled the unknown Atlantic, and removed at once and forever the fancied dangers in the way of its navigation. It destroyed the old patristic geography, and practically demonstrated the rotundity of the earth. It overthrew the old ideas of science, and gave a new meaning to the Baconian method of investigation. It revolutionized the commerce of the world, and greatly stimulated the intellect of Europe, already awakening from the long torpor of the Dark Ages. It opened the doors of a New World, through which the oppressed and overcrowded population of the Old World might enter and make homes, build states, and develop a higher ideal of freedom than the world had before conceived.

But this event did not come to pass by accident, neither was it the result of a single cause. It was the culmination of a series of events, each of which had a tendency, more or less marked, to concentrate into the close of the fifteenth century the results of an *instinct* to search over unexplored seas for unknown lands.

The fifteenth century was the period of transition from the darkness, the bondage, and the sluggishness of the Middle Ages, to the light, the liberty, and the activity of Modern Times; and the discovery of America by Columbus was the one event of all, on which this transition hinged. The series of events which brought about this change, and which awakened, fostered, and stimulated this spirit of geographical discovery and maritime enterprise, may fitly be called *the historical conditions in the Old World preparing for, and making possible the discovery of the New.* The principal of these were the *Crusades*, the travels of *Marco Polo* and others to the eastward by land, the explorations of *Prince Henry*, of Portugal, to the south and west by sea, the improvement of the *Mariner's Compass*, the *Invention of Printing*, the beginnings of the *Protestant Reformation*, and the *Political Condition of Europe* in the fifteenth century.

THE CRUSADES.

The period extending from the fifth century to the fifteenth, is known in history as the Dark Ages. It was a time of great mental and moral stagnation. The masses of Europe were in a condition of ignorance and superstition almost without a parallel since they have claimed to be at all civilized. It was a time when *might* made *right*, and when the limited experience of the individual constituted the sum of his knowledge. Everything had become local; states and individual minds, were confined within a very limited horizon. Something was needed to energize the people and to unite them in one common enterprise, to awake intellectual life, and to engender moral enthusiasm. It came in the Crusades, a series of wars between the Christians of Western Europe and the Mohammedans of Southwestern Asia.

The number of these wars, including the Children's Crusade, was eight or nine.

They occurred between the years 1095 and 1291 A. D., and the principal seat of war was in the countries bordering the eastern end of the Mediterranean Sea.

Causes.—From very early in the Christian era, pilgrimages to the various places associated with the life and death of the Savior,—especially his tomb at Jerusalem—had been regarded as acts of great piety, and had been sanctioned and encouraged by the popes and the clergy. In the seventh century the Mohammedan Arabs took Jerusalem; however, they still permitted, and even encouraged, the Christian pilgrimages. But in 1076, the Seljuk Turks, a rude and barbarous race, recently converted to Mohammedanism, and almost as ignorant of their own faith as of Christianity, captured the Holy City, compelled the pilgrims to pay large sums for the privilege of visiting the holy places, and otherwise treated them with great cruelty. The reports of returning pilgrims, and especially the preaching of Peter the Hermit, stirred all Europe with fiery indignation. The Pope saw in this a grand opportunity for realizing the unity of Catholic Christendom; and at the Council of Clermont, in 1095, he addressed a vast concourse of clergy and laymen in favor of a holy war against the Turks for the recovery of the sacred shrines. The enthusiastic cry of "God wills it, God wills it," by the multitude settled the question and became the war cry of the enterprise. Each one who enlisted wore on his shoulder the sign of the the *cross*, made of red cloth; hence the name *crusade*, from the Latin word *crux*, meaning a cross.

Some of the Facts.—Immediately all Western Europe was ablaze with enthusiasm, and in an incredibly short time a million men, women, and children were on the march toward the Holy Land. Those who first started were from the lowest grades of society. The prisons were opened and all classes of criminals were allowed their liberty and promised eternal salvation on the condition that they would join the Crusaders. These formed an ignorant and undisciplined rabble; but later, princes, nobles, and even the kings of England, France, and Germany, laid aside the reins of government, and, clad in knightly steel, led brave and brilliant armies to battle with the savage Turk and the courtly Saracen.

In 1099 Jerusalem was taken, and a Christian kingdom established, which, after a precarious existence of eighty-eight years was overthrown by the famous Saladin, and was never re-established.

During the period of these wars the Crusaders fought in southeastern Europe, Asia Minor, Syria, Palestine, and Egypt; but on the fall of Acre, the Ptolemais of Scripture, in 1291, the Crusades came to an end.

Effects.—1. They tended to break up the *Feudal System*, and to disseminate popular freedom by compelling the feudal lords to sell their lands in order to furnish troops and supplies for the wars, and by inducing the kings to grant political privileges to cities in return for contributions of money. In this way a class of persons who had been vassals before, were lifted into a condition of greater independence of thought and action.

2. They brought the Crusaders into contact with two civilizations—the Greek and the Saracenic—both of which were older, richer, and more advanced than their own. Thus their knowledge was greatly increased; progress in science, literature, and art was promoted; and a general stirring up of men's minds was produced. The old stationary state of things in Europe was closed by the Crusades.

3. They brought the masses into closer communication with the clergy, and the amount of selfishness and corruption discovered in their spiritual advisors destroyed much of that superstitious belief in the purity and infallibility of the church. This broke the spiritual shackles with which Rome had so long held her subjects in bondage, and roused in the people that freedom of thought, and hardihood of opinion, which finally resulted in the Protestant Reformation.

4. They vastly increased geographical knowledge, and created a passion for travel.

5. They encouraged maritime enterprise in the following ways :

a. By improving the quality and increasing the number of ships. This resulted from the necessity of transporting large armies and their supplies across the Mediterranean Sea to the seat of war.

b. By increasing the number of trained seamen.

c. By bringing distant nations into communication with each other and teaching them the benefits of a mutual exchange of products.

d.   By increasing the wealth of certain cities of Italy, making them the commercial centres of Europe, and giving them control of the Mediterranean Sea, and the lines of traffic with the East. This created in the growing states of Western Europe, a desire for like commercial advantage ; but as the lines of traffic had fallen into the hands of the Italians, the other states must look in a different direction ; hence, there arose pre-eminently, a desire for a southern or a western route to the rich trading marts of the Indies.

From what has been said, it may be seen that the effects of the Crusades not only tended to make the discovery of America possible, but, with some other causes, actually led to that result.

EARLY TRAVELERS.

The Crusades created an intense desire for travel, which a few adventurous spirits very early gratified. We shall notice some of these and the relations which their travels bore to the discovery of America by Columbus.

Among the first was one *Benjamin*, a Spanish Jew, who, about 1160, started from Saragossa, and traveled through Italy and Greece to Palestine. He then turned his steps toward the countries bordering on the Black and Caspian Seas, and thence to Chinese Barbary. He next traversed the countries of Farther India, embarked on the Indian Ocean, visited its islands, and after thirteen years came back to Europe with a great amount of information, which was circulated as his "Notes of Foreign Lands." These were widely copied, (there being no printing then) and wonderfully inflamed the spirit of adventure.

But greater than the Jew was the Venitian, *Marco Polo*,

who set out about one hundred five years after Benjamin's great journey. His family were of the nobility, and engaged extensively in commerce. His father and his uncle, in the prosecution of their traffic had visited Tartary, and their stories kindled in his mind a desire to become a traveler whose field should be wider than that of any of his predecessors. Fortunately, at the age of eighteen, circumstances favored the accomplishment of his purpose, and in 1265 he began his journey. His father and uncle had visited the court of Kublai Khan, and gained his confidence. The Khan sent them back to the western powers to negotiate treaties, one of the officers of his court accompanying them. With this embassy young Marco returned. The Khan was pleased with his youthful guest and enrolled him among the attendants of honor. He was soon employed in confidential missions, and held this relation to the Khan during seventeen years. At length he became a trader in the Indian Ocean, and for twenty-six years he continued his commercial pursuits in the chief centres of Asia. He was often beyond the limit to which any European had ventured. He traded with the merchants of the extreme east of Asia, visiting Japan, the existence of which was not even suspected by Europeans. Commerce had never before had such an explorer. He returned to Italy the wonder of mankind. The people stood amazed at his descriptions of vast regions of opulence, fertility, power, and glory,—regions the names of which were like those of romance.

Polo wrote a minute description of his journey, which produced a startling effect upon the mind of Europe, inflaming it with an unwonted interest in the golden regions of Asia.

Everywhere an Asiatic turn was given to trade. Asia was the subject of thought, of conversation, of dreams, of trade, and of speculation. "His work was of inestimable value as a stimulant and guide to geographical research; it encouraged the Portuguese to find the way to Hindoostan round the Cape of Good Hope; and it roused the passion for discovery in the breast of Columbus, thus leading to the two greatest of modern geographical discoveries."

This book of Polo's furnished the data from which the German geographers constructed improved maps and globes; but unfortunately, (or fortunately) Polo had made no astronomical observations, nor had he even recorded the length of the day at any place; hence the geographers, who had no certain data for estimating the extent of the countries which he had traversed, propagated errors which led to results that were destined to influence the history of mankind. They incorporated on their maps and globes, their own rough estimates of Marco Polo's day's journeys, making the distance traveled much greater than it really was. They thus represented the continent of Asia as extending across the Pacific Ocean, and having its eastern shores somewhere in the region of the West Indies. These erroneous calculations led Columbus to the false assumption that by sailing west a comparatively short distance he would come to the wealthy trading marts of China. As a result of this conviction he entered upon that memorable expedition which terminated in the discovery of the continent of America.

The next traveler of importance, was *Sir John Mandeville,* who left England in 1322. Passing through France, he proceeded to Palestine where he joined the army of the Turks.

He afterward served under the Sultan in Egypt, and in southern China under the Khan of Cathay. He resided three years at the great city of Pekin, and then, after traveling over a large part of Asia, he returned to England, having been absent more than thirty years. He wrote a book of his travels, which was copied in several languages. This book gave a more detailed description of those countries than any previous work had given. It thus served to extend the knowledge of the people who could afford to possess it, and to keep up the interest in travels and traffic in the East.

But these travelers whom we have named went by land; they could only report of those countries that are linked together, forming the Eastern Continent. They could tell nothing of America, and but little of Africa. To gain a knowledge of these countries required greater advancement in *maritime enterprise*. For this advancement, much of the honor is due to Prince Henry of Portugal.

PRINCE HENRY THE NAVIGATOR.

"The mystery which for ages had hung over the Atlantic, and had hidden from the knowledge men, one-half of the surface of the globe, had reserved a field of noble enterprise for Prince Henry of Portugal. Until his time the pathways of mankind had been the mountain, the river, and the plain, the strait, the lake, and the inland sea; but it was he who first conceived the plan of opening a road through the unexplored ocean, a road replete with danger but abundant in promise."

This remarkable man was the son of King John I. of Portugal, and Queen Philippa, daughter of John of Gaunt, Duke of Lancaster. He was born in Oporto in 1394. He has been

styled "The Navigator;" also "The Father of Modern Geographical Discoveries," and he well deserves these honorable
titles. At a very early age he distinguished himself in the
wars against the Moors; and in the prosecution of these wars
he went into Northern Africa, where he learned many new
and strange things about that country and its people. Thus
originated the great ambition of his life, to find a sea-path to
the Indies by circumnavigating Africa. This path till then
was known only through faint echoes of almost forgotten
tradition.

To be duly appreciated this thought must be viewed in
relation to the time in which it was conceived. The fifteenth
century has been rightly named the "last of the Dark Ages,"
but the light which displaced its obscurity had not yet begun
to dawn when Prince Henry, with prophetic instinct, traced
in his imagination a pathway to India by an anticipated Cape
of Good Hope. No printing-press as yet gave forth to the
world the accumulated wisdom and experience of the past.
The compass, though known and in use, had not yet embold-
ened men to leave the shore and put out with confidence into
the open sea: no sea-chart existed to guide the mariner along
the perilous African coasts; no light-house reared its stately
head and spread the light of its friendly eye to warn or wel-
come him on his dreary track. The scientific and practical
appliances which were to render possible the discovery of
half a world, had yet to be developed. But, with these
objects in view, Henry took up his residence at Sagres, near
Cape St. Vincent, the extreme southwestern point of Portugal. It was an inhospitable place. Another spot so cold, so
barren, so dreary, it would be difficult to find in sunny

Portugal. But it suited his purposes; it furnished good harborage, and three-quarters of the horizon were occupied by the mighty and mysterious waters of the as yet unmeasured Atlantic. Here he devoted a number of years to the incessant study of mathematics, astronomy, cosmography, cartography, and navigation. He drew around him the chief men of science; and that their learning might be made practically useful, he established an observatory and a school of navigation, in which the known facts of geography were reduced from their former crude shape into an intelligible system. With princely liberality of reward he invited the cooperation of the boldest and most skillful navigators of every country. He built arsenals and dock-yards; improved the skill and stimulated the industry of his shipwrights; the mariner's compass was brought into use as it had never been before; and his pupils and seamen were taught how to determine latitude and longitude by means of astronomical observations. Much improvement was likewise made in the construction of maps and charts; for the beginning of which work he diligently collected the information supplied by ancient geographers, and new material was constantly accruing from reports brought back by the numerous expeditions fitted out to explore the African coast and to collect authentic information concerning it.

Henry had learned from the Moors concerning the rich gold coast of Guinea, and he determined to reach it by water. His first expedition was sent out about the year 1415. This is remarkable as being *the first expedition for discovery sent out by any nation in modern times*, and it is no less remarkable that it was planned and executed by a youth who had scarcely reached the age of manhood.

Cape Nun, (or Non, meaning *not*) lies between Portugal and the Guinea Coast. Previous to Henry's time this cape had been regarded as the farthest point of the earth. Beyond it, superstition had pictured a realm of spectres, and the boldest mariners could not be induced to attempt its passage. The Portuguese had a proverb running thus: "Whoever passes Cape Non will return or *not*." This cape, however, was doubled, and at a distance of sixty leagues beyond, the more stormy and dangerous cape, Bojador, was reached. For twenty years attempt after attempt was made to pass it, but in vain. About the year 1420, two of Henry's boldest seamen, Zarco and Vaz, in making this attempt were swept by the fury of the gales out to the open sea. Here, as the storm continued, they lost their bearings and surrendered themselves to despair; but fortunately they were driven into the haven of a distant island, which, in gratitude they named, Porto Santo, i. e., Holy Haven. This voyage marks in navigation, the abandonment of the old method of coasting, and the commencement of a new style of sea-faring, that of stretching boldly out into the ocean. These men were compelled in returning home, to trust the compass, and finding it trustworthy, they were now ready to pass any of the stormy capes by standing far out from the shore. In 1434—1436, Cape Bojador was doubled by Gil Eannes. Seamen were now becoming educated to a bolder navigation, and voyage succeeded voyage in rapid succession, each crew returning with abundant evidence of the possibility of navigating waters which had hitherto been considered impracticable.

The island reached by Zarco and Vaz was one of the Madeiras. Three hundred miles from the coast, the Cape Verde Islands were found, and *nine* hundred miles from any continent a single vessel reached the Azores. The darkness of superstition was giving way before the light of Prince Henry's operations. Intense excitement prevailed. Thinking men everywhere were amazed at the revelations so rapidly made. From all quarters sailors came to find employment, and students to obtain instruction, under the wonderful Prince. For a time Henry bore all the expense of these voyages himself, but when discoveries became popular, and the merchants found that there was profit in the expeditions, self-supporting societies were formed under Henry's patronage and guidance. The government, too, furnished aid, and what began in the faith and enthusiasm of a single individual, became the passion of a whole nation.

In 1460, in the midst of his successes, Prince Henry died; but his mantle fell upon his brother, King John II. of Portugal, who was in every way worthy to become his successor. In 1471 the Portuguese had crossed the equator, finding the coast of Africa, which superstition had pictured under a belt of fire, not only habitable, but very fertile, and already populous. Finally one of John's expeditions reached the Cape of Good Hope, and the route to India by the south and east was opened to the world.

There is little doubt that Columbus had been fired by the travels of Benjamin, Marco Polo, and Sir John Mandeville; the news of the Portuguese successes added fuel to the flame; and in 1470 he came to Lisbon in search of employment and geographical knowledge, as many others had already done. Here he married the daughter of one who had been a great sea captain under Prince Henry. With his wife, Columbus

obtained possession of many valuable maps, charts, and
instruments of navigation. He was appointed governor of
the Madeira Islands, which had been colonized soon after
their discovery. It was while living here that he matured
his theory of the form of the earth, and of a western route to
India; and it was here that his theory was greatly strength-
ened by learning that there had been found on the western
coast of the Azores and Cape Verde Islands, pieces of strangely
carved wood, trees, seeds, and the bodies of two men whose
color and features were different from any familiar to Europeans at that time. He could no longer forbear to test his
theory; he therefore returned to Europe for aid. His diffi-
culties in obtaining it need no repetition here.

While the operations of Henry and John were not directed
toward America, it is easy to see that they were steps in the
preparation for its discovery. "If from the pinnacle of our
present knowledge, we mark on the world of waters those
bright tracks which, during the last four centuries and a half,
have led to the discovery of mighty continents, we shall find
them all lead us back to that same inhospitable point of Sagres,
and to the motive which gave to it a royal inhabitant." A
long lifetime after Henry's plan was first laid, Columbus succeeded in accomplishing that stupendous achievement which
formed the connecting link between the Old World and the
New; and while to Columbus belongs the highest honor of
this great benefaction to the world, it should never be forgotten that the explorations of Prince Henry of Portugal, .
were in reality the anvil upon which that link was forged.

Of Henry's work, Irving beautifully says, ' It was effected,
not by arms, but by arts; not by the stratagems of a cabinet,

but by the wisdom of a *college*. It was the great achievement of a prince who has been well described as being full of thoughts of lofty enterprise, and acts of generous spirit,—one who bore for his device the magnanimous motto, 'The talent to do good;'—the only talent (desire) worthy the ambition of princes."

THE MARINER'S COMPASS.

The world is probably indebted to the Chinese for a knowledge of the directive power of the magnet, and to the Arabs for its introduction into Europe. The magnet is said to have derived its name from magnesia, the country in Asia Minor, where the lodestone was first found. The Chinese annals assign the invention of the compass to the year 2634 B. C., when they say the emperor Houangti constructed an instrument for indicating the south. At first it seems to have been used exclusively for guidance in traveling by land. Humboldt says that one of the Chinese emperors in the eleventh century B. C., presented to the ambassadors at his court from Tunkin and Cochin China, "magnetic cars," that they might not miss their way on their return home. The earliest mention that we have of their using it by sea, is about the year 300 A. D.

The directive power of the magnet seems to have been unknown in Europe until late in the twelfth century A. D. The first mention of it in any European writing is in a treatise by Alexander Neckam in 1180. It was mentioned also in a satirical poem leveled at the Pope in 1190 by the French poet Guyot de Provins. We quote it from Goodrich's "History of the Sea."

"As for our Father the Pope,
I would he were like the star
Which moves not. Very well see it
The sailors who are on the watch.
By this star they go and come,
And hold their course and their way.
They call it the Polar Star.
It is fixed, very unchangeable :
All the others move,
And alter their places and turn,
But this star moves not.
They make a contrivance which cannot lie,
By the virtue of the magnet.
An ugly and brownish stone,
To which iron spontaneously joins itself
They have ; and they observe the right point.
After they have caused a needle to touch it,
And placed it in a rush : (straw)
They put it in the water without anything more,
And the rush keeps it on the surface :
Then it turns its point direct
Towards the star with such certainty,
That no man will ever have any doubt of it :
Nor will it ever for anything go false.
When the sea is dark and hazy,
That they can neither see star nor moon,
Then they place a light by the needle,
And so they have no fear of going wrong :
Towards the star goes the point,
Whereby the mariners have the skill
To keep the right way.
It is an art which cannot fail."

But the most interesting reference to the magnet in this connection, before the needle was set on a pivot in a box, is by Brunetto Latini, the teacher of Dante, who visited the philosopher Roger Bacon at Oxford, England, in 1258. We quote from Major's "Prince Henry the Navigator:"

"The Parliament being summoned to assemble at Oxford, I

did not fail to see Friar Bacon as soon as I arrived, and
(among other things) he showed me a black ugly stone, called
a magnet, which has the surprising property of drawing iron
to it ; and upon which if a needle be rubbed, and afterward
fastened to a straw, so that it shall swim upon water, the
needle will instantly turn toward the Pole-star: therefore, be
the night ever so dark, so that neither moon nor star be visible, yet shall the mariner be able, by the help of this needle,
to steer his vessel aright. This discovery, which appears useful in so great a degree to all who travel by sea, must remain
concealed until other times ; because *no master-mariner dares
to use it* lest he should fall under a supposition of his being
a magician ; nor would even the sailors venture themselves
out to sea under his command, if he took with him an instrument which carries so great an appearance of being constructed
under the influence of some infernal spirit. A time may
come when these prejudices, which are of such great hin-
drance to researches into the secrets of nature, will probably be
no more ; and it will be then that mankind shall reap the
benefit of the labors of such learned men as Friar Bacon, and
do justice to that industry and intelligence for which he and
they now meet with no other return than obloquy and
reproach."

It is difficult, from the conflicting and fragmentary accounts,
to determine just when the magnet ceased to be an article of
curiosity, as it was in Bacon's time, and became one of practical and reliable use. Most writers assume that the change
occurred when the needle was poised on a pivot and enclosed
in a box. But when this was, and by whom it was done, is a
matter of doubt. It is supposed, however, that this was done

by Flavio Gioja, (pron. Jŏ-ya) about the beginning of the fourteenth century. Whether this is true or not, it is certain that Prince Henry urged his men to use it and to trust it, and it was known and used effectively in the voyages made under his direction. The poising of the needle on a pivot, was the beginning of a new era in navigation. Previously the mariner was careful to keep within sight of the shores and head-lands along which he coasted, thus often making his voyage long, tedious, and dangerous; but after some experience in testing the certainty of the directive power of the compass, he felt that he had a safe guide to his movements, and with this assurance he bade adieu to the stars, promontories, and coasts which formerly had been his close companions, and pushed boldly out into the open sea. Without the compass it is not at all probable that even the daring mind of Columbus would have ventured to brave the dangers of the dark, stormy, and mysterious Atlantic.

THE ART OF PRINTING.

The honor of bringing this art to that degree of perfection which made it of such wonderful benefit to mankind, is claimed by both the Dutch and the Germans. By the former, it is claimed for Lawrence Coster (or Koster) between the years 1420 and 1426; by the latter, for John Gutenberg, between 1440 and 1450. The names of John Faust (or Fust) and Peter Schœffer also appear in the history of printing, with some claims to honor; but they were capitalists furnishing means, and not the thinkers who perfected the work.

Gutenberg's claims are best established, and to him, most writers on the subject assign the invention. His invention was not that of printing with movable types, for that had

long been known in Europe. It was known and practiced
by the Chinese probably five-hundred years before Gutenberg's time. His work was the invention of the type mold,
by which metallic types could be rapidly and accurately produced. So complete was this invention when it left his hand,
that it is the only method of type making now in use, not having been materially improved from that day to this. Previous
to Gutenberg's discovery, every letter was engraved by hand
on the types, and consequently book-making on an extensive
scale by the use of such types was practically impossible.
Like many other benefactors who preceded and followed him,
Gutenberg was thought crazy and visionary by his contem-
poraries; but like Galileo, Columbus, Stephenson, and Good-
year, he felt that there was laid upon him the accomplishment
of a work which was to prove a benefaction to the world.
This feeling, and a sublime faith in his ability to perform it,
sustained him under discouragements which would have
crushed a mind uninspired by such ideas as inspired him.

This invention was exceedingly opportune. It was made at
a time when men's minds were awakening from the lethargic
sleep of the Dark Ages; when there was an intense desire to
know more of the world; when a few truly scientific men
were investigating the laws and forces of nature in a systematic way; and when men were beginning to think for themselves in religion as well as in science. Printing was needed to
preserve and disseminate the results of these investigations.
If Gutenberg had preceded the American discoveries of the
Norsemen, and printing had been in as general use then as it
was in 1492, the world would not have needed the services
of a Columbus. By means of the press Columbus was enabled

to accumulate sufficient material from the travels of Polo
and others, from the published works of the German geographers, and from the reports of the Portuguese discoveries, to
construct his theory of the form and size of the earth, and of
a western route to India. Printing is the "art preservative of
all arts." By it each generation is enriched by the accumulated wisdom of all the past.

> "Mightiest of all the mighty means,
> On which the arm of *progress* leans,
> Man's noblest mission to advance,
> His woes assuage, his weal enhance,
> His rights enforce, his wrongs redress,
> *Mightiest of the mighty is the Press.*"

THE PROTESTANT REFORMATION.

The Reformation was that great spiritual and ecclesiastical
reform which took place in Europe during the fourteenth,
fifteenth, and sixteenth centuries, and which divided the
Roman Catholic Church into two great opposing parties,
finally resulting in the establishment of the various ecclesiastical denominations of Protestant Christendom. Before
1492 the main principles upon which this reform proceeded
had been preached among the Waldenses in Southern France,
by Wickliffe in England, by Huss in Bohemia, and by Savonarola in Italy. Although the separation in the church did
not take place until early in the sixteenth century, the way
had been prepared by these great preachers and others more
humble, so that when Luther took up the work he needed
only to gather together into a form the elements that had
been made ready for him.

Causes.

1. *The Crusades.* They brought the common people and
the clergy into closer relations, and the people saw, to some

extent at least, the degraded state of affairs in the church, and the cloud of mystery which had so long hung over the chair of St. Peter, filling the nations with awe, was partially dispelled.

2. *Invention of Printing.* This brought about a general diffusion of knowledge by reducing the cost of books, thus enabling the poorer classes to profit by the translations of the Bible, and by the thoughts of the leading men of the day.

3. *Establishment of Universities.* The organization of universities in various parts of Europe, threw many great scholars into the midst of the people. In 1453 Constantinople fell into the hands of the Turks, when large numbers of learned Greeks found their way as teachers into these schools, and gave a wonderful impulse to freedom of thought.

4. *Immorality of the Clergy.* The clergy as a class, had lost all ecclesiastical discipline, and all sorts of crimes were common among them. They became luxurious and ambitious; and, as the revenue of each was too little for his avarice, it became the fashion to seize that of others,—to pillage, assault, and oppress inferiors.

5. *Illegal Election of Pope Urban VI.* This election, which occurred toward the close of the fourteenth century, caused the dissatisfied cardinals to elect Robert, cardinal of Geneva, under the title of Pope Clement VII. Europe was about equally divided in support of the two claimants. From this period the power of the Pope declined. For forty years after this there were constantly two, and sometimes three popes, each claiming to be the head of the church, and each denying the infallibility of the others. Councils were assembled which endeavored to settle the disputes and to determine the true pope. These councils claimed jurisdiction above the popes.

6. *The sale of Indulgences.* The immediate cause of the reformation was the sale of indulgences. The system of indulgences as first practiced, consisted in the imposing by the church of certain good works as a partial substitute for certain offenses. The payment of sums of money was gradually substituted for the performance of the good works. This money was at first regarded as alms, of which the church was to be the dispenser; finally, it was received for the purpose of gratifying the extravagance and avarice of the popes. Plenary indulgences were not granted until the time of the Crusades. When the popes had established the practice of selling these indulgences, it became the means of taxing all Christendom. The agents who sold them used every means to insure success in their sale. Tetzel, one of these agents, boasted of saving more souls from hell than St. Peter had converted.

Effects.

1. *Intellectual.* The Reformation was favorable to the development of intellect. The Roman Catholic Church substituted the decrees of the popes and councils for the judgment of the individual. The Reformation proceeded upon the principle of free inquiry in matters of religion, which would naturally lead to free inquiry in matters of science as well. This freedom of thought began early to make breaches in the wall by which the church had sought to circumscribe the investigations of science. It over-turned the old Ptolemaic theory of geography, and established the more rational one, accepted, and afterward proved by Columbus.

2. *Change within the Church.* This outside pressure caused a reform within the church itself. It became purer in its practices, and changed materially, its attitude toward science,

especially those branches of it which had to do with geography and navigation.

3. *It augmented the power of Kings.* Before the Reformation began, kings and other rulers were held subject to the papal authority. Now, they were, in a measure, their own masters. This gave them freedom to engage in maritime and other enterprises without consulting the wishes of the papacy. Not only this, the breaking up of the excessive sale of indulgences, left more money to be applied to these enterprises.

POLITICAL CONDITION OF EUROPE IN THE FIFTEENTH CENTURY.

From the breaking up of the Roman Empire in the fifth century, to the time of the Crusades in the twelfth and thirteenth centuries, the political condition of Europe was chaotic. The *feudal system* was at its height, and a great number of petty kings and nobles ruled the masses and quarreled with one another. During this time there existed, of course, little idea of nationality; but through the influence, chiefly, of the Crusades, the feudal system was broken up; the stronger kings overcame the weaker; power and territory were consolidated; and by the middle of the fifteenth century the modern states of Europe were pretty well established. The leading of these were Italy, Spain, France, Portugal, and England.

It will be remembered that the Crusades gave to certain Italian cities great commercial prominence. Italy, therefore, of all these ambitious young nations, held the first place in wealth and power. Her cities were rich, her navigators skillful, her navies powerful, and the entire trade of Western Europe with the East was in her hands. The other nations, finding themselves commercially tributary to her, and seeing that her commerce was the key to her prosperity and power, became jealous of her, and began to devise ways and means to out-rival her; and as she firmly held the old caravan routes to the Indies, the only way in which they could hope to succeed was by finding a new road by water.

Soon after the conquest of Constantinople by the Turks in 1453, these same Turks took possession of the over-land routes to India, and as a result, the Italian trade with the East was almost entirely destroyed. Now, Europe must forego the luxuries of the East, or find a new way to get them. It was readily seen that the nation that should first secure the new route would hold the same relation to the others that Italy had previously held, and the struggle began in earnest.

Up to this time the western nations had accomplished little for want of skillful navigators, but the destruction of Italian commerce had thrown out of employment such men as Columbus, Verrazzani, and the Cabots, who were soon found sailing under the patronage respectively, of Spain, France, and England; and for whom, while seeking a western passage to the rich trading marts of India, they founded claims to territory in America.

Thus the political condition of Europe in the fifteenth century brought about a struggle for increased political power through commercial supremacy, which promoted maritime enterprise, and led immediately to the discovery of the New World.

This chain of events preparing for the discovery of America, is an illustration of the great truth that all history is but the development of a plan. Each event accomplished is a step in its realization. Man goes forward in the execution of a design which he has not himself conceived, and which, it may be, he does not understand. It is not until it manifests itself in outward realities, and he has reached the elevated vantage ground of some series of great achievements, that he is able to recognize and comprehend it. Until the modern era there was no just recognition of the continuity of human events, no true appreciation of the movement of history, nor any well defined confidence in the future. The wonderful developments in science, art, and literature, and the imposing procession of events in the unfoldings of human history in all its phases, are but the harmonious expression of a great organic thought. It is by man himself, by the development of his intellectual powers, his sensibility, and his will; in short, by coming into the conscious possession of his inheritance,—true rational freedom, that the great scheme of the world is accomplished. A comprehension of this fact reveals to man the dignity of his position in the economy of history. He to whom this thought commends itself, will be reconciled to the past through the lessons it teaches him, he will be content to do in the present the duties which it brings to him, and he will have an abiding faith, and a cheerful confidence in the developments of the future.

www.ingramcontent.com/pod-product-compliance
Lightning Source LLC
Chambersburg PA
CBHW021413090426
42742CB00009B/1135

* 9 7 8 3 3 3 7 3 8 1 2 6 4 *